Canmore & Kananaskis
History Explorer

by Ernie Lakusta

Altitude Publishing
The Canadian Rockies/Vancouver/Colorado

Publication Information

Altitude Publishing Canada Ltd.
The Canadian Rockies
1500 Railway Avenue
Canmore, Alberta T1W 1P6

www.altitudepublishing.com

Copyright 2002 © Ernie Lakusta

Canadian Cataloguing in Publication Data
Lakusta, Ernie
Canmore and Kananaskis History Explorer
(SuperGuide)
Includes index.
ISBN 1-55153-633-1 (pbk.)

1. Canmore (Alta.)--History. 2. Kananaskis Country (Alta.)--History. 3. Canmore (Alta.)--Guidebooks. 4. Kananaskis Country (Alta.)--Guidebooks. I. Title.
FC3699.C35L34 2002   971.23'32   2002-910868-3
F1079.5.C355L34 2002

Altitude GreenTree Program
Altitude Publishing will plant in Canada twice as many trees as were used in the manufacturing of this product.

Project Development

Layout	Hermien Schuttenbeld
	Scott Manktelow
Illustrations/maps	Scott Manktelow
Editor	Andrea Murphy
Index	Elizabeth Bell

Made in Western Canada
Printed and bound in Canada
by Friesen Printers, Altona, Manitoba

We acknowledge the financial support of the Government of Canada through the Book Publishing Industry Development Program (BPIDP) for our publishing activities.

A Note from the Publisher
The world described in *Altitude SuperGuides* is a unique and fascinating place. It is a world filled with surprise and discovery, beauty and enjoyment, questions and answers. It is a world of people, cities, landscapes, animals and wilderness as seen through the eyes of those who live in, work with, and care for this world. The process of describing this world is also a means of defining ourselves.

It is also a world of relationship, where people derive their meaning from a deep and abiding contact with the land—as well as from each other. And it is this sense of relationship that guides all of us at Altitude to ensure that these places continue to survive and evolve in the decades ahead.

Altitude SuperGuides are books intended to be used, as much as read. Like the world they describe, *Altitude SuperGuides* are evolving, adapting and growing. Please write to us with your comments and observations, and we will do our best to incorporate your ideas into future editions of these books.

Stephen Hutchings
Publisher

Table of Contents

Preface

Kananaskis Country welcome sign on Highway 40

This book is an introduction to the history and lore of Canmore and Kananaskis Country. In it, you will read about the legendary explorers, historical accounts, place names, cultural history, legends, and even the mythological and fictitious events that form the fascinating historical background to this beautiful region. It is not a guidebook to the hiking trails or scrambles in Canmore or Kananaskis Country. Excellent references exist for just those purposes.

The mountains and surroundings of Canmore and Kananaskis Country are rich in history. Every mountain, river, stream, and valley has a story to tell. Reading this book, you will be introduced to World War I commanders and battle cruisers, war heroes, vicious battles, intrepid explorers, mythological creatures, and heroic guides and climbers.

This information should interest people from all walks of life and of varied interests. The hiker and climber will enjoy some of these stories as much as the average tourist, who will finally be able to locate, identify and learn of the history associated with this area.

My first encounter with Kananaskis Country was in the late 1960s, when I was a graduate student at the University of Calgary. My research gave me the opportunity to investigate the Kananaskis Lakes, Highwood Pass, Evan-Thomas Creek, Sibbald Flat, and Powderface Ridge regions of the region. At this time the dreaded drive on the Forestry Trunk Road, begun in 1948 and completed in 1952, was a bone-jarring, white-knuckle, dust-choking drive, but the compensation was the magnificent scenery, flora, fauna, and solitude of the region. Kananaskis has become a part of me ever since those early days.

Anyone who can remember that drive certainly appreciates the easy access we have to the park today. I have to confess that I was one of the skeptics who resented turning this beautiful region into a recreational area accessed by a major highway. Later, I came to the realization that the Kananaskis belonged to everyone, not just the lucky few who hiked and backpacked into the area.

When it comes to the history of the region, the contribution made by members of the First Nations has unfortunately been largely ignored. Very little of the Stoney history of the area has been recorded, and yet the Stoney have been associated with these mountains for many generations. I have tried to incorporate much of their fascinating legend into this book, and I hope readers will become more aware of the role they play in the history of the Kananaskis Valley. Perhaps their legends will be taken into account and future place names in the Kananaskis will reflect this rich heritage.

The subject matter has been arranged in geographical sections according to major rivers and valleys that serve as routes into Canmore and Kananaskis Country. This arrangement should make it easier for those travelling into the region to become familiar with its mountains and lore. Major routes into Kananaskis Country are the Trans-Canada Highway, Elbow Falls Trail (Hwy. 66), Sibbald Creek Trail (Hwy. 68), Kananaskis Trail (Hwy. 40), or the Smith-Dorrien/Spray Trail (Hwy. 742). The mountains associated with these routes are identified at specific sites on an illustrative map (page 6) and presented as panoramas that can be consulted by the reader. Sometimes mountains are difficult for the novice to identify. They can look completely different, depending on whether they are viewed from the front or the back. In order to overcome this problem, different views of the same mountain from different routes into the Kananaskis are presented wherever possible.

In each section of the book a general history of the region is presented. Photographs of major vistas taken from specific viewpoints along these major routes will then allow you to identify mountain peaks and the historical events associated with their names.

Each year, thousands of new visitors flock to this beautiful area. They, too, will be able to say, "I know the name of that mountain", or, "Did you know that mountain was named after a famous naval battle of World War I?" And hikers or scramblers stuck in a tent on a rainy day will now have something else to read!

Finally, some of the information in this book may encourage the reader to become more aware of the natural history of the area and conscious of the need to preserve the natural beauty and heritage of Canmore and Kananaskis Country.

For information on the nearby Banff/Lake Louise area of Banff National Park, the reader is referred to Ernie Lakusta's Banff and Lake Louise History Explorer, published by Altitude Publishing. Mr. Lakusta follows the routes of the early explorers as they make their way through the Canadian Rockies wilderness, naming the countless peaks, valleys, rivers and lakes as they go. This book reveals the stories behind the names and scenes of this famous region.

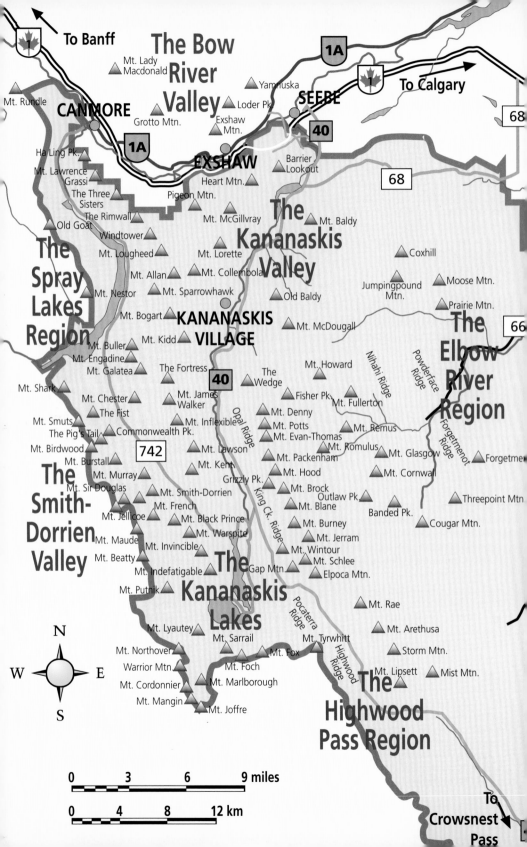

Kananaskis Country

Creation of Kananaskis Country

Mountains are great apostles of nature whose sermons are avalanches and whose voice is that of one crying in the wilderness.
Longfellow, 1836

Alberta's Kananaskis Country, a multi-use provincial recreation area, is located on the eastern slopes of the Rocky Mountains. Its western boundary adjoins Banff National Park, running down the Continental Divide to its southern boundary, which is marked by Highway 732. The Trans-Canada Highway delineates the northern boundary, while the eastern boundary coincides with the Bow-Crow Forest Reserve. Within the boundaries of Kananaskis Country are seven provincial parks and many regions designated as wilderness areas.

The creation of Kananaskis Country has had a long and, some might say, trying history. The eastern slopes have always attracted attention because of their beauty and diverse ecology. For these reasons, in 1902 the region was made part of Rocky Mountain Park, which eventually became Banff National Park. It was withdrawn from the national park in 1911, but placed within it again in 1917.

In 1930 the Canadian government passed the National Parks Act, which set a new standard for the nature and quality of land set aside as national parks. Lands not conforming to this act were withdrawn from Banff National Park. Forest fires in the

Opal Range in Kananaskis Country

Kananaskis Valley that had scarred its landscape, proposed hydroelectric projects in the Spray Lakes district, and logging practice in the Kananaskis region resulted in the permanent removal of Kananaskis Country from Banff National Park. The Kananaskis region became part of the Rocky Mountains Forest Reserve, administered by the Dominion Forestry Service. The Alberta Department of Lands and Mines assumed control of its natural resources in 1930, and this led to the formation of the Eastern Rockies Forest Conservation Board, with its focus on conservation and forest resource management. When the Alberta government published 'A Policy for Resource Management of the Eastern Slopes' in 1977, the concept of Kananaskis Country was born, and the rest is history.

Kananaskis Country, one of the world's most beautiful and spectacular recreational systems, was the ambitious project of Premier Peter Lougheed and the Minister of Recreation, Parks and Wildlife, Red Adair. In 1975, Premier Lougheed announced the creation of Kananaskis Provincial Park, to be centred on the Kananaskis Lakes region, with an area of approximately 208 square kilometres. (Later, in 1986, this became Peter Lougheed Provincial Park.) That area was expanded in 1977 to its present size with the creation of Kananaskis Country as a multi-use recreational area. The magnificent landscape of Kananaskis Country consists of over 4000 square kilometres of prairie, foothills, mountains, glaciers and snowfields, and includes the drainage systems of seven sparkling rivers.

Kananaskis: What's in a Name?

The exact origin of the name Kananaskis is unknown, but it is steeped in the legend of the valley. Captain John Palliser named the valley, river, and pass in 1858 after an Indian, "of whom there is a legend, giving an account of his most wonderful recovery from the blow of an axe, which had stunned but had failed to kill him." According to the legend, Kananaskis was hit by the axe in a battle near the present-day Kananaskis Ranger Station in an area known as Brulé Flats. In Palliser's printed report and James Hector's papers the name is spelled 'Kananaskis', but various other spellings crop up in the literature, such as 'Kannaenaskis', 'Kinnonaskis' and 'Kananaskasis'. Lt. Thomas Blakiston, another member of Palliser's expedition, was known to use the term "Kananaski" to refer to the same area.

Whatever the origin of the name of the river, the valley, and the lakes, it is a fact that in the Stoney language the Kananaskis Lakes were known as *Ozada Imni*, or 'Valley Lakes', while the Kananaskis River was known as *Mini thni-ozada*, or 'Tributary of the Cold Water River' (referring to today's Bow River).

While Palliser is responsible for naming the Kananaskis valley, river and pass, he was not the first person of European descent to enter the area. As far as we know, that honour goes to James Sinclair (see pages 128-30), who first explored the valley in 1841. In that year Sinclair secured the services of a young Cree chief of the Wetaskiwin band known as Mackipictoon, and together they led a group of settlers up the Kananaskis Valley and across North Kananaskis Pass bound for the disputed Oregon Territory.

Building the Rocky Mountains

These mountains are our sacred places. They are our temples, our sanctuaries, and our resting places. They are places of hope, a place of vision, a place of refuge, a very special and holy place where the Great Spirit speaks with us.

Chief John Snow

Mount Yamnuska, showing the McConnell Fault

In 1787, a young David Thompson wrote in his journal:"The Rocky Mountains came in sight like shining white clouds on the horizon. As we proceeded they rose in height; their immense masses of snow appeared above the clouds forming an impassable barrier, even to an eagle."

Come west from Calgary. Leave the plains, cross the foothills and behold the limestone rock faces that were deposited up to 570 million years ago. Little on the skyline has changed since David Thompson wrote those words. These are the Rocky Mountains, born on ancient sea floors. They dominate the horizon, forming one of the longest continental ranges in the world. Kananaskis Country is part of the eastern slopes of these mountains.

As you leave the foothills region on the Trans-Canada Highway, you will be leaving sandstone rocks that are quite young—only 75 to 130 million years old. But as you drive west and leave Scott Lake Hill, you will be confronted with the striking feature of the McConnell Fault. The Rocky Mountains begin at this junction between the foothills and the front ranges, where the McConnell Fault has thrust much older Eldon limestones up and over younger sandstones of the Belly River Formation. This major fault is evident in the rock composing Mount Yamnuska, on the north side of the Trans-Canada Highway at the entrance to the Bow Valley.

How did the mountains form? Why are there places where older rocks lie on top of younger ones? What titanic forces can move mountains?

The Legend of the Formation of the Mountains

There is an old legend, variations of which are common to many Indian tribes, regarding the creation of the earth and mountains. Eons ago, the earth was an empty place without mountains, hills, or prairies, only a great sea as far as one could see. A mythical creature called *Wi-suk-i-tshak,* or Old Man, who was part man, part god, and part sun, was unhappy with this situation as he floated endlessly across the water on a raft with all manner of animals, looking for land.

Finally tiring of looking, Old Man asked the loon to dive in search of mud from which he could make some land. The loon was unsuccessful. The muskrat then tried, but the water was too deep and again no mud was found. Finally the beaver tried. He was gone for a long time, and when hopes of finding him began to fade, he floated to the surface exhausted

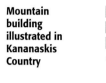

Mountain building illustrated in Kananaskis Country

	Sandstone & Mudstone
	Limestone & Dolomite
	Crystalline Basement
	Thrust Fault

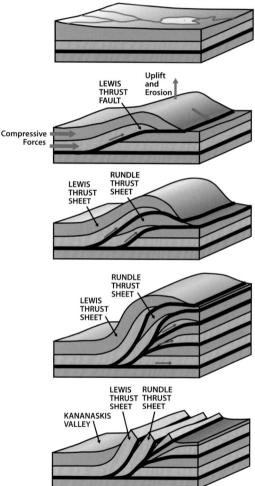

covered them with grass, trees, and all manner of flowers and animals. Finally, he created man, and taught him to live with the aid of nature. And that is how the Rocky Mountains were formed.

What Really Happened? Moving Continents!

The Cause of Uplifting

All the mountains we are viewing were formed by the uplifting of ancient sea floors, caused by the movement of tectonic plates. The North American continent is actually floating on the denser, flowing rock of the mantle layer beneath the crust of the earth. These crustal layers are termed tectonic plates. When stress occurs between the mantle and the crust, gigantic movements take place to relieve this stress. Tectonic plates move at imperceptible rates of about five centimetres per century.

We are sitting on the North American Plate, which is moving westward. At the same time, at this very moment, the North American Plate is crashing into the Pacific Plate, which is moving eastward. As these two plates collide, the resulting pressure causes folding and faulting. Sedimentary rock is forced up onto the Pacific Plate, which is actually sliding under the North American Plate. It is this 'up-piling' of rock that formed the Rocky Mountains.

Geologists refer to periods of mountain building as orogenies, two of which are responsible for the mountains we see in Kananaskis Country. The main ranges, including the Fairholme and Kananaskis ranges, were formed 175 million years ago during the Columbian Orogeny. The front ranges, consisting of the Opal and Fisher ranges as well as the foothills, were thrust upward by what geologists refer to as the Laramide Orogeny.

and half-unconscious. When Old Man lifted him onto the raft, he noticed that the beaver clutched a ball of mud in his tiny paw.

Old Man took the mud and with it he made the earth. Piling up heaps of mud he created the Great Backbone, and so created the mountains and all of the peaks of the Great Divide. He also made the level prairies, and then

Folding and Faulting

A fault is a crack or a break in the earth's crust along which rocks move. The majority of faults along the eastern slopes of the Rockies are called thrust faults. These are faults that have resulted from compression of the crust that forces sediments up and over the fault, as can be seen in the photo of Mt. Yamnuska. Faulted rocks are then subject to differential erosion by the action of glaciers, water, and wind.

A fold is a bend or warp in the earth's crust. Enormous pressures and extremely high temperatures can combine to cause soft sedimentary rock to buckle or fold. Almost every type of fold is possible, and many are represented in the mountains of Kananaskis Country.

Shaping the Mountains

No sooner had these mountain ranges formed than nature started to tear them down. The forces of erosion have gradually worn down the mountains and sculpted them into their present shapes. Agents of erosion include chemical action, the force of running water, and the alternate freezing and thawing of frost and ice.

Mangin Glacier from King Creek Ridge

Then, approximately two million years ago during what geologists call the Pleistocene Epoch, a great sheet of glacial ice advanced over most of western Canada. The effect of this glacial action shaped the topography of the mountains and formed the valleys we see today. No other force has had such a profound influence on the shape of the Rocky Mountains. Although these glaciers began to recede over 10,000 years ago, the small glaciers present in Kananaskis Country are reminders of this glaciated past.

Glaciers in Kananaskis Country

The many small glaciers that can be found in Kananaskis Country only occupy about 15 km2 or 0.3% of the region. Most are found in Peter Lougheed Provincial Park, in the cirques and valleys close to the Continental Divide. The Mangin Glacier is the largest, occupying 493 hectares, and it has the distinction of being the southernmost glacier in the Rocky Mountains of Alberta.

Names and sizes of glaciers within Peter Lougheed Provincial Park.	
Glacier Name	**Area (hectares)**
Mangin	493
Haig	270
Mt. Northover	130
Mt. Smith-Dorrien	100
Mt. Robinson	90
Mt. Beatty	73
Mt. Foch	65
Mt. French	50
Lyautey	40
Mt. Lyautey East	32
Mt. Sarrail	24
Mt. Marlborough	24
Mt. Lyautey North	12

The castellate appearance of Mount Kidd

Mount Murray, a horn mountain

The actions of wind and water have combined to create the jagged sawtooth formations of the Opal Range

Mount Birdwood, a typical dogtooth mountain

Many mountains of the Kananaskis Range are examples of overthrust, or, as they are more commonly called, "dip slope" mountains.

Major Shapes of Mountains in the Kananaskis

Castellate Mountains

Castellate mountains are formed when alternating bands of hard and soft rock erode in such a way as to form vertical cliff faces between ledges.

Horn Mountains

The action of glacial ice over long periods of time is responsible for carving out bowl-shaped depressions (known as cirques) into the face of certain mountains. Over time, this action results in an isolated tower or horn.

Sawtooth Mountains

Great compressive forces cause the rock strata to bend vertically. Erosional forces then break down the rock, creating gullies between separate summits, which resemble the teeth of a saw.

Dogtooth Mountains

When tremendous forces cause the rock to be thrust up almost vertically, the forces of erosion wear away the softer rock, leaving the more resistant rock in the shape of spires, characteristic of the Opal Range.

Overthrust Mountains

Great horizontal compressive forces result in rock strata being thrust up over much younger rock, tilted at an angle of 20 to 40 degrees. Over time, glacial action slowly cuts across the horizontal layers of rock, causing them to slide away as huge talus slopes. This reduces the 'dip slope' angle of the strata and produces the characteristic southwesterly 'dip', giving these mountains their characteristic writing-desk shape.

Life Zones in Kananaskis Country

A unique set of abiotic and biotic interactions has resulted in many diverse ecosystems in Kananaskis Country, and biologists have recognized five distinct ecoregions in the park. An ecoregion describes "an area characterized by a distinctive regional climate as expressed by its vegetation" (Sub-committee on Biophysical Land Classification, 1969).

The five distinct ecoregions present within Kananaskis Country are the Alpine, Subalpine, Montane, Boreal Foothills, and Aspen Parkland. Climatic factors such as soil type, slope angle and exposure, precipitation, and altitude are the primary factors influencing the structure and distribution of vegetation in each ecoregion. Visitors will be made aware of these factors as they explore Kananaskis Country.

The subalpine is a glorious place to visit in the autumn

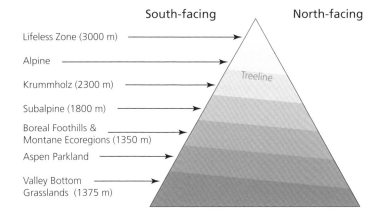

Ecoregions: This diagram can be used as a hypothetical guide to the distribution of the various ecoregions in Kananaskis Country, controlled by slope angle, aspect, and altitude..

Who Named these Peaks?

What's in a name? Have you ever wondered how a mountain or natural landmark came by its name? The process is not a haphazard one. The Geographic Board of Canada was created in 1897 to standardize principles to be followed in the naming of landmarks. Today this same board is known as the Canadian Permanent Committee on Geographical Names. The first guidelines established that geographical names should be a reminder of the history of the region. When future generations inquire about a name, it should awaken memories of the history that produced it, and lead to an appreciation of our natural landmarks. Historical figures or events can be used to name a mountain, but should not supercede local history. Once a name has been proposed, it is then up to the committee to make the name official.

In actual fact, anyone can submit a name to Alberta's Geographical Names Programme for consideration. In practice, however, very few individuals or groups are actually involved in the first stages of naming a mountain. Once a name has been proposed, it is then up to the Canadian Permanent Committee on Geographical Names to make it official.

The following individuals or groups have been responsible for the naming of most of the mountains in Kananaskis Country.

Native People

The Stoney Indians had names for most of the mountains in Kananaskis Country. Native people understood the importance of naming geographical locations as reference points for travel. Their names reflected unusual physical features or memorable events associated with the landmarks in question. Lamentably, most of these names have been forgotten. Surveyors and engineers replaced them with names of little local historical significance. In this book, whenever possible, the original Stoney name will be given for each mountain or landmark described, with a literal translation, and then the origin of the official name. Yamnuska and Nihahi are Stoney names that have been accepted by the Geographical Names Board of Canada. Sadly, most of their other names have been overlooked or discarded by the committee. There are still a number of unnamed peaks in the Kananaskis region and it is strongly urged that, where possible, future names reflect the culture and history of the aboriginal people of the area.

The Palliser Expedition

Members of the Palliser Expedition—Captain John Palliser, Eugène Bourgeau, James Hector and Thomas Blakiston—produced some of the first detailed maps of the Kananaskis region and are responsible for the naming of many of its features. Long before guidelines had been set for the naming of mountains, members of the expedition chose names reflecting the appearance, natural phenomena, or history of the region. Kananaskis Pass itself and Grotto and Cascade Mountains are but a few examples. Other names, such as the Livingstone Range and Mount Fox, were chosen to honour respected scientists and explorers.

George Mercer Dawson (1849–1901)

Who was George Mercer Dawson? He was a giant of his times and the pioneer geologist of western Canada. In 1884 and 1885, Dawson trekked through vast tracts of the largely uncharted territory of Alberta and British Columbia with the Geological Survey of Canada, making detailed and precise observations on the geology, meteorology, ethnology and flora. This he accomplished with boundless enthusiasm, despite a serious physical handicap. Dawson named many of the mountains during his explorations in the Kananaskis region. To his credit, the names he chose reflected natural features or historical accounts of western Canada.

A Debilitating Childhood Disease

When Dawson was nine years old, he began to experience the effects of a childhood spinal illness called Pott's disease, which is tuberculosis of the spine. It arrested his growth and left him with a permanently twisted and curved back. Dawson would never attain more than the stature of a ten-year-old, and he would always have a hunchback. During his long and slow recovery period, he was educated by tutors and his father. He later attended Montreal High School and McGill University before going to England, where he graduated from the Royal School of Mines with the highest marks in his class. He overcame his handicap and became one of the leading authorities on the geology and natural history of Western Canada.

Dawson the Distinguished Scientist

Dawson became a member of the International Boundary Commission, which, between 1873 and 1875, surveyed the 49th parallel from Lake of the Woods to the Rockies. He then joined the Geological Survey of Canada, surveying across the prairies, through northern British Columbia and the Yukon, travelling as far north as the Bering Sea.

He spent two summers in the Rockies. His first summer involved mapping the mountains from the 49th parallel to the headwaters of the Oldman River and then up the Columbia valley to present-day Golden. From there he made his way east through the Kicking Horse Pass and then down the Bow Valley to Calgary. The second summer he mapped the mineral resources of the Kananaskis Valley from the Bow River to the headwaters of the Kananaskis River and from Mount Assiniboine (which he named) north to Kicking Horse Pass.

Dawson was appointed director of the Geological Survey of Canada in 1895, and as his fame spread, he was appointed president of the Geological Society of America in 1896. He died in his fifty-second year in 1901 from an acute case of bronchitis. Today every map of Canada bears honour to his name. Dawson City and the Dawson Mountain Range in the Yukon, Dawson Creek in British Columbia, a bay in Manitoba and a glacier in British Columbia are witness to this man's enormous achievements. But, as Joyce Barkhouse so aptly put it, "Perhaps George would be most pleased that he is remembered by a tiny species of mouse, named in his honour, whose descendants still scamper freely across the tundra of the Far North."

George Mercer Dawson, the assistant director of the Canadian Geological Survey, in 1885

A.O. Wheeler
(1860–1945)

Arthur Wheeler, surveyor, writer, climber, and map maker, was a native of Kilkenny, Ireland, and arrived in Canada in 1876. He was in charge of the Boundary Commission, which, during the years 1913 through 1924, was delineating the provincial boundary between Alberta and British Columbia. This arduous task involved the detailed mapping of the border along the 1,000-kilometre-long Continental Divide.

It was during his survey work with the Boundary Commission that Wheeler received permission from the Geographic Board of Canada to name the peaks in and around the Kananaskis Lakes region. He mapped the Kananaskis region using the new photographic survey method developed by Dr. Edouard Deville, Surveyor General of Canada. Using this new technique, the Boundary Commission set up 120 camera stations on these mountains and developed 765 photographs for topographic purposes.

A.O. Wheeler, the "Grand Old Man of the Mountains"

Of the forty-four peaks in what is now Peter Lougheed Provincial Park, Wheeler named thirty-eight, and probably chose names for many others. Unfortunately, he disregarded the first mandate of naming mountains, which was to reflect the natural history of the area, and in a fit of patriotism named most of the mountains surrounding the Upper Kananaskis Lake after World War I generals. Within the Kananaskis Lakes region, he wrote in 1916, "are many striking peaks, five of which are over 10,000 feet and two over 9,900 feet in altitude; they are all dominated by the great peak named Mt. Joffre and have been given the names of distinguished generals who have rendered such names immortal through their splendid services to France in the great war now in progress."

Later, on the advice of Wheeler, many other peaks in the Highwood Pass region and the Opal Range were named after British admirals and even British warships that took part in the Battle of Jutland during World War I.

It is important to remember the lessons of history and the efforts and sacrifices of the millions affected by war, but what do the names of generals (many of dubious merit), admirals (many with debatable credentials), and battleships tell us of the history of the Rockies? R.M. Patterson, in *The Buffalo Head* (1961), probably said it best: "The Rockies must sadly be the worst-named range in the world!"

Grand Old Man of the Mountains

Wheeler, with Elizabeth Parker, co-founded the Alpine Club of Canada in 1906, serving as its first president from 1906 to 1910. He was personally responsible for setting up the annual club meetings at various historic sites in the mountains and he even did some trail building in the region during the 1922 Alpine Club of Canada's mountaineering camp at Palliser and North Kananaskis passes.

He was the leader of the expedition that resulted in the first ascent of Mount Robson, by Conrad Kain, Albert MacCarthy and W.W. Foster on July 30, 1913.

By most accounts, Wheeler caused his guides much grievance. They often found him to be abusive, arrogant, conceited, and autocratic. Edward Feuz Jr. once saved Wheeler's life after he had refused a rope. As Wheeler was sailing down the slope towards a 1,000-foot drop-off, Feuz jumped on top of him to arrest his fall, but thought to himself that it might have been a better idea to let him fall the whole way!

Another legendary story involved Fred Stephens, a pack train guide. After a brief exchange he said, "Mr. Wheeler, I always heard you were a son-of-a-bitch, and you are." He then promptly unloaded all of the pack animals and left Wheeler with one or two others alone at Centre Pass with a ton of supplies and no horses to carry them.

Everyone knew you had to stand up to Wheeler.

Recent Suggestions

Fortunately, nearly all of the recently-named peaks in Kananaskis Country have names that reflect the history of western Canada. Most of these were suggested by members of the Alpine Club of Canada. We now have Mount James-Walker, Calgary's Citizen of the Century, Mount Denny of the North West Mounted Police, and Mount Potts the renowned scout to glorify our skyline. We also have colourful names such as Forgetmenot, Three-point, Banded and Mist Mountains, as well as Powderface and Grizzly Ridges. What a relief! Hopefully the Committee on Geographical Names will eventually accept unofficial but colourful names such as Outlaw and Grizzly peaks.

Historical Routes into Kananaskis Country

Initially, routes into the Rocky Mountains had one purpose — to provide access to lucrative fur trade from the northwest. The Bow Corridor was the eastern approach to a number of important mountain passes that had been used by prehistoric cultures and Native peoples since time immemorial. These routes followed trails already established by the Kootenay, Snake, Blackfoot and Stoney Indians. The passes we now call Highwood, Kananaskis, Elk, and White Man were used as hunting and trading routes across the Great Divide prior to the arrival of the first European explorers.

As the dispute over the Oregon Territory intensified, the government of Canada hoped to establish its claim to the territory by sending settlers across the Great Divide. This resulted in new passes being found by James Sinclair in 1841 and again in 1854. Fear of annexation by the United States led to Warre and Vavasour being sent to explore possible routes suitable for troop deployment (see pages 133-34). By the time the Palliser Expedition arrived in western Canada, the focus was to find a route through the mountains that would be suitable for a major road and railway that would unite Canada from coast to coast.

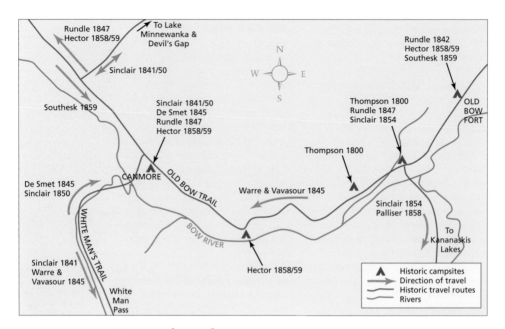

The Canmore Corridor, showing the locations of Old Bow Trail, Kananaskis Trail, Old Canmore Trail, White Man's Trail, and the early explorers who used these trails.

Routes into the Bow Valley

Devil's Gap

With the establishment of Rocky Mountain House, the first route into the Rocky Mountains followed ancient trails along the Ghost River, through Devil's Gap, and then into Lake Minnewanka Valley. This trail followed the southeast side of the lake before it branched, with one trail leading down Carrot Creek into the Bow Valley near Canmore, and the other passing down the Cascade River to rejoin the Old Bow Trail near present-day Banff. The Carrot Creek branch would be followed through Whiteman's Gap above Canmore to the Spray River and White Man Pass over the Great Divide. The Cascade River branch led to Simpson and Vermilion Passes.

Old Bow Trail

Prior to the arrival of Palliser, the Old Bow Trail left Bow Fort and followed the north side of the Bow River past its junction with the Kananaskis River.

David Thompson used this route in 1800, travelling as far as Whiteman's Gap. He and Duncan McGillivray must have viewed the future site of Canmore beneath the Three Sisters when they climbed the "inaccessible steep" near the gap. In 1845, Lieutenants Warre and Vavasour, on their way to Oregon Territory on a secret military mission, may have used this route on their way to White Man Pass. Although there is no record of travellers using this route from 1826-1834, Hudson's Bay Company personnel stationed at Old Bow Fort must surely have ventured up this corridor in search of game.

James Hector and Eugène Bourgeau, members of the Palliser Expedition, were the first to provide a detailed description of this trail when they used it in 1858 and again in 1859. Hector wrote in his diary, "Towards evening an excellent camping was reached opposite a mountain with three peaks, which forms a very imposing group. In a nearby clearing we made camp and stayed for several days making a geological study of the rock formation." In 1859 the Earl of

Southesk travelled eastward using this route, from his hunting trip in the mountains.

Routes into the Kananaskis Valley

Kananaskis Trail

This route into the Kananaskis area left Bow Trail west of the junction of the Kananaskis and Bow Rivers, fording the Kananaskis River west of present-day Seebe. It then followed the west side of the Kananaskis River to the lakes in order to avoid swampy areas in mid-valley. James Sinclair used this trail on his way to the discovery of Kananaskis Pass in 1854. Captain Palliser essentially followed this same route when he entered the valley in 1858 in search of the same pass Sinclair had discovered four years before.

Old Canmore Trail

A map prepared by George Dawson of the Geological Survey of Canada in 1886 clearly shows a trail on the south side of the Bow River from the Kananaskis River to Canmore. This trail was connected to the Kananaskis Valley via Pigeon Creek and a trail over Skogan Pass. In 1936 this trail was widened to accommodate wagons, and ran from Dead Man's Flats across Skogan Pass to the Boundary Cabin. This trail and various side trails were used by many of the coal prospectors who were exploring the valley for minerals.

Today: The Modern Trunk Road

Twenty miles of road were constructed in 1934 from Seebe to the Kananaskis Forest Experimental Station. In 1936 the first Forestry Trunk Road was built, and 'Leaping Lena', owned by Calgary Power and driven by Bob Bell, made the first automobile trip into the valley. The road to the lakes was constantly in need of repair, and ranger Joe Kovach spent most of his time maintaining the

road. It was difficult to negotiate at the best of times and proved to be a hazard for many years.

In 1948 the Alberta government commenced construction of the new Forestry Trunk Road from Coleman to Seebe, and it was officially opened in 1952. It was a good all-weather gravel road that soon enticed tourists into the valley. Upon completion, it had the distinction of being the highest engineered road in Canada where it crossed the Highwood Pass at 2206 meters (7,239 feet).

Clearing of the right-of-way for Highway 40 into Kananaskis Country began in 1973. John O'Shaughnessy was the chief engineer for its construction. He was born in Ireland and by the age of 16 was a celebrated tennis player in Europe, even playing with the King of Denmark. He worked on the Alaska Highway in the Yukon Territory, where he was buried by a rock blast. He was rescued, but his face was badly crushed and he had to undergo extensive surgery at the Mayo Clinic. He died in September 1986, at the age of 58.

The small creek feeding O'Shaughnessy Falls originates at a spring high up on the side of the mountain. This 'forever-flowing' spring was a sacred spring for the Stoneys. They called it *Mini Hniyamba Wathte Ze.* Its waters had been used for generations and it is said that neither sickness nor disease affected those who used them. To O'Shaughnessy's credit, he had the waterfall constructed to control the stream, then progressed to landscaping around the waterfall and building the wishing well that has become a favourite tourist attraction.

O'Shaughnessy Falls was named in honour of the chief engineer during the construction of Highway 40 in 1973.

The Bow River Valley

The Bow Corridor

The Bow River Valley near the "Gap" from Whitefish day use area in Bow Valley Provincial Park.

The Bow Valley corridor has been a travel route through the Rocky Mountains for thousands of years. As the glaciers retreated up the valley, hunter-gatherers of the Mummy Cave Complex, later aboriginal people, and finally the early explorers travelled this corridor. Now it's your turn to explore this route.

The 'Cold Water River'

The Bow River is over 507 km in length from its headwaters on the Continental Divide at Bow Summit to where it joins the Oldman River and becomes the South Saskatchewan River. It was known to the Stoney Indians as *Mini thni Wapta,* which means 'Cold Water River'. To the Peigan Indians it was known as *Manachabon sipi,* or 'The River where bow reeds grow'. David Thompson, who spent a winter with a Peigan band in the valley, is probably responsible for shortening the name simply to Bow River.

Prehistory

The first known human habitation of the Bow Valley took place approximately 8,000 to 10,000 years ago. Hundreds of archeological sites have been discovered in the valley. These sites were used as campsites and places where prehistoric hunters prepared their weapons. Very little is known of these hunter-gatherers, who were probably of the Mummy Cave Complex.

Hunting big game in the region, they also gathered plants for food, medicine, and ceremonial purposes. It is believed that by 2000 BC the first teepees appeared, and by AD 200 the bow and arrow as well as pottery had been developed.

Early History

The earliest known dominant tribes in the area were the Kootenay, Salish, and Snake Indians. The Snake tribe was the first to be mounted and supplied with guns, and they eventually drove the Kootenay and Salish from the valley. Unfortunately they were also the first to be decimated by a smallpox epidemic in 1780, after which the Peigan tribe, a member of the Blackfoot Confederacy, replaced them.

The Peigan never established a permanent foothold on the eastern slopes of the Rockies, and the Assiniboine Indians soon replaced them as the dominant tribe of the region. They were a peaceful people who in this area later became known as the Stoney Indians, after their way of cooking with stones. Mt. Assiniboine (3618 m), the highest peak between the international border and Banff, was named in honour of them—a fitting tribute to a proud nation.

The Arrival of the Fur Traders

Anthony Henday, an employee of the Hudson's Bay Company, was the first European to view the Rockies in 1754, but his route did not take him any nearer the mountains than Rocky Mountain House. So impressed was Henday by the mountain panorama that he coined the phrase "behold the shining mountains" in his journal.

In 1779 the North West Company was started by a group of Montreal merchants to compete with the Hudson's Bay Company for trade with the Natives. Aware of this competition, the Hudson's Bay Company sent James Gaddy to the eastern slopes to maintain their trade connections. Gaddy spent three consecutive winters with the Peigan in the foothills. Accompanying Gaddy on his third trip in 1778 was a gifted 17-year-old named David Thompson, who was destined to become western Canada's greatest map maker and explorer.

Watercolor sketch by H.J. Warre (1845) showing the route near present-day Canmore up the Bow Corridor past Mt. Rundle to Cascade Mtn.

David Thompson: Legendary Explorer and Map-Maker

The Rocky Mountains came in sight like shining white clouds on the horizon. As we proceeded, they rose in height; their immense masses of snow appeared above the clouds forming an impassable barrier, even to an eagle... About thirty miles from the mountains, we crossed the Bow River on gravel shoals near four feet in depth and two hundred yards wide.

David Thompson, on his first approach to the Rocky Mountains in 1787

David Thompson was born in London on April 30, 1770, to David and Ann Ap-Thomas, Welsh parents who changed their surname to Thompson after they moved to London. His father died when David was two years old, forcing his mother to raise him in poverty. Attending the Grey Coat Hospital, a charitable school dedicated to educating poor children in piety and virtue, he received grounding in mathematics as well as navigation in preparation for a career in the navy. That career would never come to be.

He joined the Hudson's Bay Company and began his apprenticeship to the fur trade in Canada on the shores of Hudson Bay in 1784. He was only fourteen years old and destined to become the greatest surveyor and mapmaker in Canadian history.

That first year of service was spent at Fort Prince of Wales and later at York Factory under the tutelage of Samuel Hearne. Thompson was an intelligent, pious young man who deplored the use of alcohol and tobacco. His leg was fractured in an accident in December 1788, and he was forced to convalesce for more than a year at Cumberland House. Thompson stated that the accident "turned out to be the best thing that ever happened." It was during this period that he met the accomplished surveyor Philip Turnor, from whom he expanded his mathematical knowledge and learned astronomy. In addition, he learned the use of the telescope, chronometer, and other instruments used by surveyors. This was the beginning of his career as mapmaker and surveyor. From the Peigan Indians, the previous winter, he had learned the art of surviving in the wilderness. All the more remarkable is that the following year, young Thompson lost the sight of his right eye—a major handicap for an explorer and surveyor.

In 1797, after spending fourteen years with the Hudson's Bay Company, Thompson switched allegiances and joined the North West Company. Why did he defect? Many believe it was because the North West Company better suited his lifestyle and offered him more opportunity to pursue his first passions, surveying and map-making.

Thompson married Charlotte Small in 1799, a fourteen-year-old 'child of the country' whose father, Patrick, was a partner in the North West Company. She would bear David thirteen children.

The Explorer

In 1800 Thompson met Duncan McGillivray at Rocky Mountain House and together they set off up the Bow River in search of the legendary Columbia River. Neither of them found it that year, and both retreated to Rocky Mountain House to spend the winter and contemplate further routes through the Rockies.

Thompson returned to the Rockies in 1807, determined to discover the pass over the mountains that would lead him to the great river. On June 25 he crossed Howse Pass (ironically, named for a Hudson's Bay man two years later) and found a large river, but it was flowing north. For the next four years Thompson explored the Columbia from its headwaters to the Pacific Ocean. Only then did he realize that the river had deceived him by flowing north for two hundred miles before looping back southwest to the Pacific, and that he had indeed found the Columbia.

By this time the Peigan were furious at Thompson for providing their enemies with knives, guns, and ammunition. They blocked his route over Howse Pass and threatened to kill him. In order to outwit them, Thompson began to search for another pass further north at the headwaters of the Athabasca River. On January 6, 1811, under demanding weather conditions, Thompson discovered the Athabasca Pass and the new route that would become a famous fur trade route for years to come.

Thompson left the west in 1812 at the age of forty-two, after enduring twenty-eight years of hardship in the wilderness. During his explorations he had covered over 50,000 miles on foot, by dogsled, and by canoe, mapping fully one-fifth of the North American continent. He never returned to the west, moving in 1812 to Terrebonne, near Montreal, where he set about producing maps of the country. So detailed and accurate were these maps that they were still used for more than 150 years after his death. Later, to support his rather large family, he found gainful employment with the International Boundary Commission between 1816 and 1826, surveying the Ontario section of the Canada-U.S. border.

David Thompson: Postscript

David Thompson was the greatest genius and man of all those who explored the Rocky Mountains. He was the first European to travel and map the full length of the Columbia River, yet neither a photograph nor a painting of him exists. He was the first to build a trading post on this great river. He also discovered the Athabasca Pass, a regular transportation route across the Rockies. Despite all these feats, no good biography exists of this man. The only first-hand description of David Thompson was provided by Dr. John J. Bigsby after he met the great map maker around 1850. Bigsby described him as short and compact, with long black hair that was cut square across his forehead just above the eyebrows. His "complexion was of a gardener's ruddy-brown, while the expression of his deeply furrowed features was friendly and intelligent. But his cut-short nose gave him an odd look."

Thompson was a fur trader, explorer, astronomer and cartographer, all wrapped up in the figure of a short, compact man with a friendly, weathered face. One can almost picture his long, trailing black hair flowing in the wind as he crossed Athabasca Pass. Following an eye hemorrhage, Thompson lost the sight of his only good eye and spent the last ten years of his life in total darkness. Destitute, he died in 1857. He was buried at Mount Royal Cemetery in Montreal, where his epitaph reads:

"David Thompson 1770 - 1857 To the memory of the greatest of Canadian geographers, who for 34 years explored and mapped the main travel routes between the St. Lawrence and the Pacific".

Peaks of the Fairholme Range

Mt. Yamnuska

View of 'Yam' from the entrance to Bow Valley Provincial Park

John Laurie in 1957

They may not realize that the cliffs of Yamnuska consist of 650-million-year-old sandstones faulted over 75-million-year-old rocks in what has become known as the McConnell Fault.

Hitchhiking to Banff in 1952, Hans Gmoser could hardly contain his enthusiasm when he saw the mountain for the first time. "I was fascinated. A beautiful rock face took shape. In one straight line it rose to the sky. My eyes were fastened upon it and as the mountain stood there, solemn in this May evening, a silent promise was made." Gmoser returned to Mt. Yamnuska on November 23 of that year, along with Leo Grillmair and Isabel Spreat. They completed the first ascent of its south face by a route now known as the Grillmair Chimneys. Little did Gmoser realize that he had started a new phase in Canadian mountaineering. Realizing its climbing potential, he returned to the mountain many times to put up a variety of routes on the face.

The Mountain with Three Names

To everyone in the local alpine community the mountain is known as Yamnuska, or simply 'Yam'. The name is derived from the Stoney *Iyamnatthka*, which means a flat-faced mountain or wall of stone—an apt description of the shape of the mountain. The Stoneys applied this name to the peak shortly after their arrival in the Rockies from the Lake of the Woods in Manitoba during the early 1700s. The mountain even had spiritual significance for them. (See 'The Legend of the *Yahey Wichastabi*', page 47).

In 1961 the mountain was officially named Mount John Laurie in honour of the founder of the Indian

The peaks north of the Trans-Canada Highway are not technically within the boundary of Kananaskis Country, but they are included here as they are the first peaks encountered when travelling from the east. All of these mountains belong to the Fairholme Range, which is bounded on its northern edge by Lake Minnewanka, on the south by the Bow River, and on the east by the foothills.

Palliser named the range in honor of William Fairholme, a Scottish friend who later married his oldest sister. William Fairholme's younger brother Walter was one of the men who lost their lives on the ill-fated Franklin Expedition to the Arctic. It was William Fairholme's account of a Missouri hunting trip he made in 1840 that fired Palliser's imagination and prompted him to propose his famous expedition. By coincidence, Lieutenant Henry Warre (see 'Spies in the Kananaskis', pgs 133-34) accompanied William on that hunting trip.

Mount Yamnuska (Mt. John Laurie) 2240 m

Mount Yamnuska is the first mountain one encounters when travelling west on the Trans-Canada. Travellers are held in awe by its imposing face.

Association of Alberta, who was a tireless advocate of Native rights. And so, with the stroke of a pen, the perfectly suitable Stoney name for the mountain with the flat face was replaced forever with the official 'Mount John Laurie'.

John Laurie (1899-1959)

John Laurie was a Canadian educator and political activist who was born in Ayr, Ontario on October 23, 1899. He was a graduate of Galt Collegiate Institute, the University of Toronto, and Calgary Normal School. Laurie came to Alberta in 1921, where he taught at Western Canada College from 1923-1927 and at Crescent Heights High School from 1927-1956. In 1939 he became interested in the problems facing the Indians and spent the next twenty years espousing their cause and furthering their education. In 1940, he was adopted by Stoney Chief Eons Hunter and his wife, who named him White Cloud. John Laurie acted as the Secretary of the Indian Association of Alberta from 1944 to 1956. In 1956 he was selected as Calgary's citizen of the year and had an honorary Doctor of Laws conferred on him by the University of Alberta.

Loder Peak
2097m

Loder Peak is actually a minor high point on the ridge leading to the summit of Goat Mountain (2405 m). The first minor peak on the ridge leading to Loder, termed Door Jamb Mountain, is the most probable mountain climbed by Thompson and McGillivray in 1800 when they observed the sea of peaks leading to the Great Divide.

The mountain is named after Edwin Loder, who settled in Kananaskis Country in 1880. He came to the hamlet of Kananaskis in 1884 to cut lumber for the railway, but soon became interested in the limestone kilns

operated by a Mr. McCanleish. Loder obtained employment at the plant and became so efficient that he was often left in charge of the entire plant.

On one occasion when McCanleish took a trip to Calgary, Edwin was left in charge, but McCanleish disappeared and was never heard from or seen again. An extensive search and investigation by the RCMP could not locate the owner of the plant or find any evidence of foul play.

Eventually Edwin Loder and his brother Richard obtained squatter's rights to the limestone kilns and operated the plant under the name Loder Brothers. They experienced some economic problems but finally raised enough capital, and incorporated under the name Loder Lime Co. Ltd. in 1905. With this new capital investment, three new kilns were built by 1914 to supply the growing demand for lime in western Canada.

In 1900, Edwin Loder became the first postmaster for the Kananaskis district, a post he held until 1935, and the Loder home became the social centre of the hamlet of Kananaskis.

Could this be the legendary mountain of Thompson and McGillivray?

When David Thompson returned to the Rocky Mountains in 1800 as an employee of the North West Company, he met Duncan McGillivray at Rocky Mountain House, and together with four men and a Peigan guide they entered the mountains along the

Loder Peak between Goat Mtn. (right) and Door Jamb Mtn. (left) from Whitefish day use area in Bow Valley Provincial Park

Edwin Loder in the 1930s

View of the ridge leading up Door Jamb Mountain, from the Whitefish day use area in Bow Valley Provincial Park

Bow River. On Sunday, November 30, 1800, somewhere around present-day Exshaw, they left their horses and climbed an "inaccessible steep" ridge up to the 7,000-foot level.

Many historians believe they were at Exshaw Mountain, but I find that unlikely. Near this site is where the ridge leading from Loder Peak reaches almost to the valley bottom (see photo above). This is likely the mountain Thompson climbed.

Thompson's journal entry for that day reads, "We began to ascend the mountain. We found it very steep with much loose small stones, very

Exshaw Mountain from the Lac des Arcs historical point of interest on the Trans-Canada Highway

sharp, but as we got higher and higher the loose stones became less frequent. Where the rock was solid, it was extremely rough and full of sharp points like an enormous rasp. This enabled us to mount places very steep, as the footing was good and sure, but it cut our shoes, socks, etc., all to pieces in a thrice."

Clearly, Thompson is not describing the treed summit of lowly Exshaw Mountain, which is nothing more than a stiff hike. Loder Peak is on the same side of the river described by

Thompson, and its elevation of over 6,800 feet is close to Thompson's original estimate of 7,000 feet. Compare this to the elevation of Exshaw Mountain—5,850 feet. Could the ultimate map maker have been off in his estimate by over 1,000 feet?

Thompson continues, stating, "Our view from the height to the eastward was vast and unbounded. The eye had not strength to discriminate its termination. To the westward, hills and rocks rose to our view, covered with snow. Never before did I behold so just, so perfect a resemblance to the waves of the ocean in a wintry storm."

Thompson and McGillivray spent four hours looking out on a scene of "wild and awe-inspiring grandeur." This is hardly the way one would describe the views from the top of the heavily-treed summit of Exshaw Mountain. Finally, the south-facing ridge of Loder Peak remains free of snow for most of the year, due to chinook winds, and can be snow-free even in November, when Thompson and McGillivray climbed this unknown ridge. We will probably never know for certain the exact mountain climbed by Thompson and McGillivray, but I believe Loder Peak to be the most likely.

Exshaw Mountain 1783 m

This diminutive mound of limestone rubble hardly qualifies as a mountain, and yet it has found its place in the folklore of the early exploration of the Bow River Valley. Situated directly behind the town of Exshaw, it is best viewed from Lac des Arcs across the valley on the Trans-Canada Highway. The same man who was responsible for the construction of Butchart Gardens in Victoria, B.C. started the limestone quarry at Exshaw in 1906. Sir Sanford Fleming named the mountain after his son-in-law, Lord

Exshaw. Who was Lord Exshaw and why did he deserve to have a mountain named in his honour? Ask Sir Sanford Fleming! Today this once-small plant is owned and operated by Canada Cement Lafarge, and has a capacity of over 7 million tons of cement a year.

Was this the historical mountain David Thompson and Duncan McGillivray ascended in 1800? I think it is highly improbable (see the explanation under Loder Peak), but you can draw your own conclusions by hiking to the summit of this diminutive peak to determine for yourself if the historians were correct!

Grotto Mountain 2706 m

This is another of the historical mountains mentioned in the report of the Palliser Expedition. When Captain Palliser split his expedition into three groups at Old Bow Fort in 1858, James Hector and Eugène Bourgeau continued to explore the Bow Valley westward along the Bow River in search of a suitable pass through the mountains to the Columbia River. They camped beside a series of lakes formed by an expansion of the Bow River that Bourgeau named 'Lac des Arcs' (Lake of the Bows).

On Thursday, August 12, 1858, Hector and Bourgeau approached a mountain, and Bourgeau named Grotto Mountain after the huge, high-roofed 'grotto' on the southwest side of the mountain, visible from many viewpoints along the Trans-Canada or the 1A highways. They entered this grotto, and, following a stream, scrambled up 300 vertical feet where they came across a "trickling fall several hundred feet in height, splashing in a clear pool with green mossy bank. In this they performed their morning abulations."

Grotto Mtn.

The Grotto Canyon Pictographs

A well-used trail from Highway 1A leads to the pictographs on the walls of Grotto Canyon. A wide spectrum of elements, including animal and human figures, has been painted on rock surfaces using red ochre. Absolute dating of these paintings has

Grotto Mountain from the Lac des Arcs historical point of interest on the Trans-Canada Highway (top) and from the Grassi Lakes Trail (bottom).

Grotto Mtn.

been difficult, but most experts agree that they are about 2,000 years old. Other examples of rock art have been discovered at Whiteman's Gap near upper Grassi Lake, and at Zephyr Creek. Unfortunately, as these sites become better known they have become objects of vandalism, and together with natural weathering, suggest that conservation efforts should be taken to manage and protect these historically valuable treasures.

Archaeologists agree that these paintings suggest a ceremonial or religious function, and both the Stoney and Blackfoot people regard these sites as places of great spiritual significance. The Blackfoot were so afraid of the power of pictographs that they were afraid to camp anywhere near them. The Stoney displayed a similar attitude, revering as sacred these

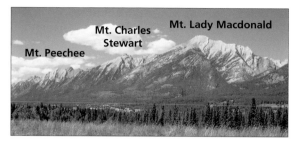

Mt. Peechee Mt. Charles Stewart Mt. Lady Macdonald

Mount Lady Macdonald from the Trans-Canada Highway near Canmore

places where the spirits wrote upon the rocks—places to be respected and feared. If you do visit any of these sites, please refrain from touching these delicate rock paintings.

The Legend of the Mako Oyadebi

Who drew these pictographs? Stoney legend states that neither the Stoney nor other Indians are responsible for these drawings. They believe them to be the work of the *Mako oyadebi*—small beings who lived underground in the mountains. These little people are very small spirits, no bigger than badgers, and are keepers of the west wind. They are gifted people with special powers bestowed on them by the *Waka taga,* the Creator, to look after the mountains and live in harmony with nature.

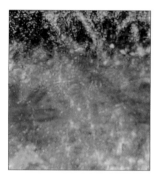

A portion of the pictographs as they appear on the walls of Grotto canyon today

Waka taga placed the little people on earth to carry out special sacred duties. One of their duties was to watch over the four sacred soils made by *Waka taga*, as these soils contain great medicines and possess great powers. The little people bring these soils up from the world below and leave them in special places for the Stoney to find and use. The four soil medicines are used in spiritual painting: rock painting, shield painting, and skin painting. The coloured soils paint the spirit of man.

Mount Lady Macdonald 2605 m

Lady Susan Agnes Macdonald was the wife of Canada's first prime minister, Sir John A. Macdonald. In 1886, shortly after the completion of the Canadian Pacific Railway, the couple celebrated this historic event by riding the train across the Great Divide to the west coast. Lady Agnes adventurously insisted on riding the locomotive's cowcatcher from Lake Louise to Golden in order to take in better views of the mountains. Although 'The Chief' thought the idea ridiculous, he relented and let her ride the cowcatcher in a makeshift seat on the front of the locomotive. As the locomotive lurched forward from Laggan, Lady Agnes triumphantly declared her vantage point to be "quite lovely" as she sat enthroned, wrapped in a linen carriage-cover. She felt "a thrill that is very like fear; but it is gone at once and I can think of nothing but the novelty, the excitement, and the fun of this mad ride in glorious sunshine and intoxicating air, with magnificent mountains before and around me." (She wrote these words about her ride for Murray's Magazine in 1887.)

Recently, it was proposed that a teahouse be built on the shoulder of Mt. Lady Macdonald, the peak named after her. It would cater to heli-hikers, offering afternoon tea. The proposal has subsequently been dropped, although the partially-constructed teahouse can still be seen on the ridge.

Mt. Lady Macdonald is one of the more popular early season scrambles in the vicinity, as it comes into condition early in the season. It is a serious hike to the summit ridge. Most hikers are stopped at once from continuing to the main summit, only metres away, by the narrow knife-edge. Only those not faint of heart continue to the summit.

James Hector (1834–1907)

James Hector was born in Edinburgh, Scotland on March 6, 1834. He graduated from Edinburgh Academy at the age of 14 and began working in his father's law office. He entered medical school at Edinburgh University when 18 years old, graduating as a medical doctor in 1856. He also took many courses in the natural sciences and was highly recommended for the position of geologist-naturalist on the Palliser Expedition by Sir Roderick Murchison, the president of the Royal Geographical Society. At age 23, Hector became the youngest member of the Palliser Expedition. (See pages 48-51 for more information about the expedition.)

In order to gather the most information possible, Palliser split the expedition into three groups. Accompanying Hector up the Bow Valley were Eugène Bourgeau, Peter Erasmus, and the Stoney Indian guide whom Hector called Nimrod, as he could not pronounce his Indian name, which meant "The one with a thumb like a blunt arrow." Erasmus became Hector's assistant and admired him for his horsemanship, physical strength, friendliness, and leadership qualities. According to Erasmus, Hector "was admired and talked about by every man that travelled with him."

Hector departed Old Bow Fort on Wednesday, August 11, 1858, on an eventful journey that would take 57 days to complete. Bourgeau stayed with the party until they reached Cascade Mtn. near present-day Banff, where he remained to botanize. Hector continued on to the Great Divide, discovering the pass now known as Kicking Horse Pass (see below), which would ultimately be the route of the transcontinental railway and highway. He took careful observations and was an excellent map maker.

George Dawson credits Hector with producing "the first really trustworthy general geological map of the interior portion of British North America."

Hector was greatly admired by the Native people for his statesmanship and his talents as a doctor. That he was able to travel through hostile Blackfoot territory without so much as one violent incident is a tribute to the great esteem in which he was held by the various Indian Nations. This 'medicine man' was given the Blackfoot name *Natoos,* meaning 'the sun'.

The Tale of Kicking Horse Pass

Perhaps the most memorable day in all of Hector's travels occurred on Sunday, August 29, 1858. On this day he not only discovered Wapta Falls, but was also kicked in the chest by his horse, and had then fallen unconscious. He had been trying to catch his horse, which had strayed off while everybody was trying to catch another horse that had fallen into the river when its pack came loose.

There are many versions of what transpired after this, but the most interesting is the story that claims Hector regained consciousness hours later, only after the other members of his party had begun to dig a grave for him. With a wink, unable to speak, he managed to save himself from being buried alive.

Today, millions of visitors each year cross the Great Divide on the Trans-Canada Highway over the same route discovered by Hector.

Before returning to England, Hector made a geological examination of Vancouver Island and toured the goldfields in British Columbia and California. In 1865 he became the Director of the Geological Survey of New Zealand, and under his guidance the entire country was surveyed.

Fifteen years after the conclusion of the Palliser Expedition, Hector was made a Companion of the Order of St. Michael and St. George and elected as a Lyell medallist by the Geographical Society. He received a knighthood in 1887.

A Final Tragedy

In 1903, at the age of 69, Sir James Hector returned to Canada with his son Douglas to revisit the Kicking Horse Pass. He joked that they were returning to visit the site of his grave, but regrettably, they never got the chance to return to his most famous discovery. His son became stricken with appendicitis and died from complications shortly after their arrival in Canada. Sir James returned immediately to New Zealand, never again to return to Canada.

A lake, a gorge, a glacier and a creek were named after him, but most fittingly, in 1884, George Dawson named splendid Mount Hector after him, to commemorate the accomplishments of this great man.

Eugène Bourgeau (1813-1877)

Eugène Bourgeau was born in Savoy in the Swiss Alps. Sir William Hooker, the first Director of the Royal Botanical Gardens at Kew, England, described Bourgeau as the "prince of botanical collectors." His excellent scientific credentials and cheerful and helpful demeanor made him an ideal choice as chief botanist for the Palliser Expedition in 1857. Palliser described Bourgeau as a "most active, energetic and excellent companion, always hard at his work in which his whole soul seems engrossed, and no matter what his fatigues or privations may be, his botanical specimens are always his first care." Palliser wrote to Sir William Hooker, "Little Bourgeau is a Brick, his collections seem to me very pretty and the colors as vivid after the specimens are saved as they are in life – He is most indefatigable and always at work."

If collecting botanical specimens was Bourgeau's specialty, horsemanship certainly wasn't. He was described as a "shocking horseman" by Palliser, and spent most of his journey travelling in uncomfortable Red River carts. This did not diminish his zeal for collecting specimens, and it was with great excitement that he viewed the prospect of botanizing in the Rocky Mountains, and the possibility of discovering scores of new specimens.

A true botanist, Bourgeau could not resist the profusion of wildflowers in the Bow Valley and the alpine slopes. Here he remained, collecting specimens for most of the summer, while Hector continued westward to discover the Kicking Horse Pass. One of his favourite sites for the collection of alpine plants was on the slopes of Mt.

Eugène Bourgeau

Lougheed, which he had named Wind Mountain for the swirling gusts that seemed ever-present on the summit.

In May 1859, Bourgeau began the long journey back to England. When he left the Palliser Expedition in 1859, Palliser paid him a fitting tribute by stating that, "In addition to his acquirements as a botanist, he united the most sociable, jovial disposition, ever ready not only to do his own work, but to assist any one else who asked him." With him he carried a preserved collection of over 60,000 plants, including 50 varieties of alpine plants that he collected at over 8,000 feet.

His companion James Hector named a splendid mountain just west of Banff to commemorate Bourgeau. It was a fitting tribute to this dedicated, cheerful, hardworking little botanist.

Peaks above Lac des Arcs

Lac des Arcs was named by Eugène Bourgeau in 1858 for the many small lakes formed by the Bow River. The peaks that border the Trans-Canada Highway above Lac des Arcs, often called the Rundle Group, run in a line from southeast to northwest from Heart Mountain to Mt. Rundle. They are found within the Canmore Corridor, bounded on the north by the Bow River.

Heart Mtn.

Heart Mountain from Highway 1A near Exshaw

Heart Mountain
2149 m

It doesn't matter whether you view this mountain from the Trans-Canada or the 1A Highway — the origin of the name is obvious. Tremendous compressive forces over 80 million years ago folded the strata into a plunging downfold that geologists call a syncline, reminiscent of the shape of a heart.

Some people think this could have been the legendary mountain Thompson and McGillivray scrambled up when they entered the Bow Valley near Lac des Arcs. The mountain is directly above Lac des Arcs and the "inaccessible steep" ridge mentioned by Thompson surely fits the north ridge of the mountain. If you have scrambled up this mountain, you know exactly what I mean! Thompson and McGillivray would have surely done some 'bum sliding' on this steep ridge. Even if they only reached the first summit that now overlooks the Trans-Canada, the elevation of approximately 6,700 feet is very close to Thompson's original estimate, and the views up and down

Mt. McGillivray

Pigeon Mtn.

As you drive west on the Trans-Canada and enter the east slopes of the Rocky Mountains through the gap blasted through the limestone rock of McConnell Ridge, this stunning view of Mount McGillivray is sure to catch your eye.

the Bow Valley are of "vast and awe-inspiring grandeur."

However, there are a number of problems with this hypothesis. First, Heart Mountain is on the south side of the Bow River, and Thompson specifically states in his journal that they were following a trail on the north side of the river. Also, the ascent of Heart Mountain does require some minor scrambling and has some route-finding problems. It is not clear whether Thompson and McGillivray would have risked serious injury due to a fall on such a ridge. No, it seems this wasn't the mysterious mountain mentioned in Thompson's journals. The more likely scenario is that they ascended Loder Peak, almost directly across the Bow Valley from Heart Mountain.

Mount McGillivray
2450 m

Who was Duncan McGillivray?
Duncan McGillivray (1770–1808) was one of three brothers of the powerful McGillivray family that originated in the highlands of Scotland. This family was one of the key stockholders in the North West Company, founded by Simon McTavish. Duncan McGillivray joined the company in 1788 and met David Thompson the following year, developing an everlasting friendship. That Thompson held his friend in great esteem is evidenced by the fact that a river, a lake, and a mountain bearing McGillivray's name appear

on maps prepared by Thompson, one of the greatest mapmakers of all time.

By 1799 both the Hudson's Bay Company and the North West Company were desperate to find the source of the great river of the west, the Columbia, which Captain Vancouver had referred to in his diaries. As a junior partner in the company, Duncan McGillivray was eager to improve his lot and immediately became interested in finding the source of this river that would provide a trade route to the Pacific and more furs for the company.

Posted to the North West's trading post at Rocky Mountain House in 1799, the tall, husky, swashbuckling McGillivray had the good fortune to spend the winter with Thompson in 1800. Eager to start, the two set off up the Bow River in late November, but with winter setting in, were forced to retreat at Lac des Arcs, near present-day Exshaw. They returned to Rocky Mountain House, where they spent the winter reading Captain Vancouver's diaries, and both became determined to find a route to the Pacific Ocean.

Did McGillivray and Thompson Cross the Rockies in 1801?
Some historians think it entirely possible that either McGillivray or Thompson or both together may have crossed the Great Divide in 1801. After all, both were stationed at Rocky Mountain House, within sight of the Rockies. Both had made forays into the valleys of the eastern slopes, and both were ambitious explorers. Why did Thompson give McGillivray's name to the present-day Kootenay River? Why did Thompson call present-day Lake Windermere Lake McGillivray? (Both of these are west of the mountains.) Why did Sir James Alexander of the Royal Engineers' Office indicate in a memo to Thompson that he should make notes on the Oregon Territory, as "He was the first

Barrier Lookout • Heart Mtn. • Mt. McGillvray • Pigeon Mtn.

to visit it from the east side of the Rocky Mountains in 1801"? Did the two men cross the Rockies in 1801? Perhaps some of the lost chapters from Thompson's journals will be found in some obscure archive and provide answers to these questions.

McGillivray was not in the best of health but that did not stop him from continuing the search for the source of the Columbia River. He pressed his reconnaissance westward, following a route along the Saskatchewan River, and finally reaching the watershed between the Brazeau and Athabasca Rivers. He saw a stream flowing west, uniting with another, and became the first European to see the tributary of the Sunwapta River. If Duncan McGillivray did cross the Great Divide during one of these expeditions, then history must also include his name in the list of great explorers of the Canadian Rockies.

Duncan McGillivray holds the distinction of being the first to present a skinned specimen of an adult male mountain sheep to the Royal Society in London. That specimen, obtained in December 1802 with Thompson, was used by Dr. George Shaw of the Royal Society as the basis for the classification of a new species, *Ovis Canadensis,* its official scientific name.

McGillivray returned to Rocky Mountain House exhausted and ill with the beginnings of rheumatic fever. His exploring days were at an end. In 1802, sick with the fever and on crutches, he left for the east, but not before developing plans for Thompson to search for the source of the Columbia. McGillivray died in Montreal in April 1808 without ever knowing that his great friend David Thompson had finally succeeded in finding the source of the great river. Without a doubt, Duncan McGillivray was a pioneer and explorer of a stature comparable to that of Simon Fraser and David Thompson.

Pigeon Mountain 2394 m

The story regarding the origin of the name of Pigeon Mountain is not terribly exciting. During the Palliser Expedition in 1858, Eugène Bourgeau named the mountain '*Pic des Pigeons*', apparently for a large flock of wild pigeons seen around the base of the mountain in the area of Lac des Arcs.

The first ascent of the northeast buttress, by G. Crocker and H. Gude, occurred in October 1967, and C. Perry and J. Martin made the first ascent of the north buttress in August 1977. If you feel like climbing the mountain, the back side sports an easy trail to the summit.

Pigeon Mountain and adjacent peaks from the exit ramp to Stewart Creek on the Trans-Canada Highway

Mt. Lougheed   I

II

IV   III

The Windtower

The four peaks of Mount Lougheed (centre to left) and The Windtower (right), from the historical sign on the Trans-Canada Highway at Dead Man's Flats

Mt. Lougheed 3105 m

Mount Lougheed consists of four identifiable peaks, three of which exceed 3000 metres. Eugène Bourgeau of the Palliser Expedition originally named it 'Wind Mountain', but this name now only applies to a minor peak some 2 kilometres north of the middle summit. In 1928 the mountain was renamed in honour of Sir James Lougheed (1854–1925), a prominent Calgary lawyer whose grandson Peter was to become premier of Alberta from 1971 to 1985.

James Lougheed, who worked in partnership with future Prime Minister R.B. Bennett, was appointed to the Senate in 1889. He was Minister Without Portfolio from 1911-1917, Minister of Soldier's Civil Establishment from 1918-1920, and Minister of Mines from 1920-1921.

First ascent of the main northwest peak was in 1889 by W.S. Drewry and A. St. Cyr. Tom Wilson claimed to have climbed the peak two days earlier, but this is unsubstantiated. The first traverse of the four peaks from south to north, by D. Gardner and N. Liske, occurred in 1967.

Sir James Alexander Lougheed

Dead Man's Flats

One of the best sites to view Mt. Lougheed is at Dead Man's Flats on the Trans-Canada Highway. Have you ever driven by this site and wondered about the origin of the name? The story is about a bone-chilling murder that occurred in the valley in 1904.

A French immigrant named John Marret owned a small homestead on the flats near the base of Pigeon Mountain. He sent for his brother François to join him and work at Canmore in the mines. François arrived in the winter of 1901, helping his brother with the delivery of milk from the homestead, but constantly complained of the pain in his head and the whirring noises threatening to take his life.

On May 10, 1904, François borrowed a double-edged axe from the Loder family and bludgeoned his brother to death while he slept. He then went to bed, and when unable to waken his brother the next morning, went to the mine and asked a friend to take John's shift because his brother was dead. François was immediately taken into custody, tried, and found not guilty by reason of insanity. He was committed to an insane asylum in Ponoka. Since that time the beautiful area where the gruesome murder took place has been known as Dead Man's Flats.

The Windtower
2697 m

The Windtower is an awesome sight from the Trans-Canada Highway. It received its name from the ever-present west winds that blow across West Wind Pass down into Wind Valley. It is hard to believe that from the back side of this mountain, it is just an easy scramble to the summit. The first ascent of the peak is unknown.

The Rimwall
2680 m

The name of this mountain is very descriptive, referring to the wall of cliffs that rims the entire summit of the peak. Just like the Windtower, this mountain also has an easy back side for scramblers. There is no recorded first ascent of the mountain.

Wind Ridge
(2164 m)

The Legend of Chinook Wind
The Stoney called this ridge *Ganutha impa,* meaning 'Windy Ridge'. Eugène Bourgeau was not the only person to experience the winds blasting through Wind Valley, across the ridge, and over the slopes of 'Wind Mountain'. Anyone who has hiked in the area finds it hard to escape these westerly and chinook winds, which keep the valley free of snow for much of the year.

According to an old Native legend, the home of these warm chinook winds is the slopes of Cascade Mountain near Banff. Chinook Wind was the name of the beautiful but blind daughter of South Wind. The wicked North Wind had carried her father away from her family many years ago.

Pigeon Mtn. The Rimwall Wind Ridge

Every now and then Chinook Wind, who longed for her father, would venture from her home on the slopes of Cascade Mountain in search of him. She would blow down the slopes of the mountain and up the Bow Valley, melting the snow on her way. This is said to be the origin of the chinook winds that blow across the eastern

West of Lac des Arcs, the Rimwall can be seen in the 'V' formed between the west ridge of Pigeon Mountain and Wind Ridge.

The Windtower

slopes of the mountains and foothills, warming the climate in the middle of winter.

Wind Ridge was also the hiding place of a Stoney brave who stole a horse and a Crow Indian maiden. Eventually the Crows tracked him down and retrieved both the horse and the maiden. The Stoney brave barely escaped from them by sliding down the opposite side of the mountain into Stewart Creek and then the safety of the Bow Valley.

The Windtower from Dead Man's Flats

The Nor'Westers

Shooting the Rapids, an oil painting by Frances Anne Hopkins (1838-1919), depicts one of the great canoes used by the North West Company.

The North West Company was formed in Montreal in 1779 as a rival to the Hudson's Bay Company and its monopoly of the fur trade in Rupert's Land. Simon McTavish, one of the Scottish co-founders, could rely on relatives such as Simon Fraser, Joseph McGillivray and many of the McTavish clan to help build a commercial empire across North America against great odds and hardships.

One of the earliest voyageurs to join the North West Company with one share was Peter Pond. Pond was everything a fur trader should be. He was taught to live off the land by the Indians, and his thoughtfulness and intelligence inspired loyalty from his staff. Misfortune dogged him, however. Two unusual murders were linked to Pond, but charges were eventually dropped due to lack of evidence. Eventually, in 1787, he sold his share in the company to William McGillivray.

In 1788, a young trader named Alexander Mackenzie joined the Nor'Westers, and at the tender age of twenty-nine became the first European to cross North America. After five tortuous years he reached the coast of British Columbia on July 26, 1793. Mackenzie left the company for a brief period of time, founding the XY Company, but was enticed back in 1804 with the merger of the XY Company with the North West Company. This merger proved to be most lucrative and put the North West Company on a direct collision course with the Hudson's Bay Company.

David Thompson, who had been employed by the Hudson's Bay Company for thirteen years, joined the Nor'Westers in the summer of 1779 for reasons still unknown. Perhaps better pay and benefits were an enticement to switch companies. He became a full partner in the North West Company in 1804, by which time it had emerged supreme in the trading wars.

Violence Results in Merger

Competition with the Hudson's Bay Company became fierce, resulting in deceit, many violent clashes and even murder. Finally in 1821, to end the dispute, Simon McGillivray signed an agreement on behalf of the Nor'Westers, combining the two companies. The two would share equally in putting up capital and would divide the profits or losses equally. Under this new agreement Sir George Simpson made certain that only the Hudson's Bay Company's name would be used, and so the end came to the North West Company name. By 1824 Simpson was fully in control of this new merger and was responsible for strengthening the company's position and Britain's claim to what would become the western provinces.

And so the life of this great company came to an end. Never again will we see courageous explorers such as Simon McTavish, Peter Pond, Alexander Mackenzie, Simon Fraser, David Thompson, or William and Duncan McGillivray under the employ of one company!

Peaks above Canmore

Though the area has been inhabited for 11,000 years, the town of Canmore wasn't founded until 1884. Canmore boasts a collection of dramatic mountains, including its signature Three Sisters.

Big Sister (2936 m), Middle Sister (2769 m), and Little Sister (2694 m)

James Hector recognized these peaks when he explored the Bow Corridor in 1858, simply referring to them as 'The Three Peaks'. Albert Rogers, nephew of CPR surveyor Major A.B. Rogers, recalls telling Canon H. Tully Montgomery of Banff on a train ride from Calgary in 1921 that the mountains looked "the same as they did one morning in September 1883 when we camped just west of what is now called Canmore. There had been quite a heavy snowstorm in the night, and when we looked out of the tent I noticed each of the three peaks had a heavy veil of snow on the north side, and I said to the boys, 'Look at the three nuns!' They were called the Three Nuns for quite a while, but later were called the Three Sisters — more Protestant-like, I suppose." This claim seems to be substantiated by the fact that the name 'Three Sisters' appears on George Dawson's Coal Basin Map of 1886, although he gave no mention as to the origin of the name.

Yet another story claims that George Stewart, first superintendent of Rocky Mountain Park, named the mountain for his three daughters, but this claim is completely unfounded.

J.J. McArthur first ascended the Big Sister in 1887. The more technical ascent of Little Sister did not occur until Lawrence Grassi led A.W. Drin-nan, M.D. Geddes, and T.B. Moffat to the summit in 1925. Middle Sister was first climbed solo in August 1921 by M.B. Morrow. Today, Middle Sister is an easy and popular scramble, while Big Sister is a more difficult one.

Mount Lawrence Grassi 2685 m

Until recently, this mountain looming above the town of Canmore was unnamed. It was officially named Mt. Lawrence Grassi in honour of the legendary resident of Canmore. If ever a peak was deserving of a name, this is it!

The Legend of Lawrence Grassi (1890–1980)

Lawrence Grassi was a miner, an amateur guide, a mountaineer, and a trail builder. He was born in Falmenta, Italy, and immigrated to Canada in 1912. His first jobs were with the Canadian Pacific Railway and then with Canmore Mines as a miner from 1916-1945.

Grassi was a distinguished climber who became one of the most accomplished and admired guides of his time, and he never charged his clients a fee! The mountain closest to his heart was Mt. Louis near Banff, which he climbed "just thirty-two times." As Grassi was very unassuming, no one will ever know exactly how many first ascents can be attributed to him. Many of his solo routes were never recorded. For Grassi, it was enough to know that he had climbed the mountain, without signing a register to

Lawrence Grassi, Ken Betts and Doug Sadler on the summit of Big Sister in 1930

The Ship's Prow

Mt. Lawrence Grassi

Ha Ling Pk.

Lawrence Grassi massif from the off-ramp at the junction of the Trans-Canada and 1A highways

Alpine Club of Canada in 1926 at the age of 36. He has been praised in the House of Commons and received the Alberta Achievement Award, but perhaps the crowning achievement was the naming of Mt. Lawrence Grassi, the peak overlooking Canmore, in his honour.

The Ship's Prow

Using technical aid, Chic Scot and L. McKay were the first to climb the Ship's Prow, a buttress of Mt. Lawrence Grassi, in July 1965 via the very prominent knife-edge ridge.

Ha Ling Peak 2680 m

claim an ascent.

Stories of his strength are legendary. He once carried an injured climber on his back for two miles down from the summit of Mt. Bastion, across a glacier to a rescue party. On another occasion he climbed Mt. Sir Donald five times on successive days during the 1932 Alpine Club of Canada camp.

Originally called the 'Beehive' and then 'Chinaman's Peak', Ha Ling Peak has had an interesting if somewhat controversial history. Ha Ling, a Chinese cook from Canmore, was bet fifty dollars that he could not climb to the summit and back to the town in ten hours. Apparently only Ha Ling knew that an easy route existed on the back side of the mountain. Starting at 7 A.M., Ha Ling climbed this route, planted a small flag on the summit, and was back in Canmore in time for lunch. No one believed his feat, and refused to pay the bet, as they could not see the flag. So the next morning Ha Ling led a group of doubters to the summit and placed a 12-foot flagpole next to his little flag, which was "proudly flapping in the wind." The peak was henceforth known as Chinaman's Peak. This name fell out of favour, and in 1998 the name was officially changed to Ha Ling Peak in honour of its first conqueror.

Ha Ling Pk.

The imposing face of Ha Ling Peak, from the same off-ramp

Grassi the Trail Builder

The quality, quantity, and design of the trails constructed by Grassi are unmatched. His first trails were constructed in Canmore in 1921, from his house to Twin Lakes (now known as Grassi Lakes), which lie beneath the towering face of Ha Ling Peak. But he is best known for his exquisite work at Lake O'Hara, where he constructed trails to Lake McArthur and Odaray Plateau, as well as the shoreline trail around the lake.

In honour of his achievements, Grassi was made a life member of the

The imposing north face of Ha Ling Peak from Whiteman's Gap was first climbed by B. Greenwood, D. Raubach, G. Prinz, and T.B. Moffat in 1961. Since that time this face has been a draw for rock climbers and has seen its share of casualties.

East End of Rundle
2590 m (EEOR)

The Rundle massif is a classic example of a 'dip-slope' mountain, and forms a long ridge approximately twelve kilometres in length. It has seven distinct peaks, the highest of which, at 2949 m, is the third peak southeast of Banff. The East End of Rundle, or 'EEOR', as it is commonly called, is the only of its peaks that lies within Kananaskis Country, forming the extreme northwest boundary with Banff National Park. The notch between EEOR and Ha Ling Peak is Whiteman's Gap, the narrow gap through which Mackipictoon guided James Sinclair's party in 1841 (see page 129).

J.J. McArthur made the first ascent of the highest summit of Mount Rundle (2949 m) in 1888. The first traverse of the Rundle massif, accomplished by C. Locke and D. Gardiner in December 1964, took three days to complete. Today the buttress at the east end is a highly popular climbing area, sporting routes with names such as Reprobate, Geriatric, and Balzac, while EEOR has become one of the more popular scrambles in the Canmore area.

Who was Reverend Robert Rundle?

Mount Rundle was originally named 'Terrace Mountain' by James Hector, but Palliser renamed it in honour of Wesleyan missionary Reverend Robert T. Rundle, in recognition of the enormous influence he had on the Stoney Indians in converting them to Christianity. Rundle worked ceaselessly among the Native people from 1840 to 1848.

Reverend Rundle arrived at Fort Edmonton on October 17, 1840. He travelled long distances to visit Cree and Stoney Indian encampments, where he gave them Christian religious instruction and also instructed them in writing.

Rundle had a passion for the mountains. He found it a magnificent spectacle "to see them painted on the western sky at sunset." One of his "never to be forgotten" Sunday services with a congregation of Assiniboine Indians was in the midst of the mountain splendour near present-day Banff. He even attempted a little mountain climbing, but his leather-soled boots impeded his progress on the loose rocks. Hungry, exhausted, and feeling faint, he was forced to abandon his attempt with the summit still far above him. Mountain climbing was not so easy after all!

Reverend Rundle suffered many hardships and had many accidents during his stay in the west. In 1848, ill health finally forced him to leave the country he so dearly loved, and he died six years later in his native Scotland. Perhaps the greatest tribute to Rundle came from the Indians he so loved: "Poor he came among us, and poor he went away, leaving us rich."

The Rundle massif with EEOR on the left, viewed from the same off-ramp

The Reverend R.T. Rundle

The Town of Canmore

Little Sister   Middle Sister   Big Sister

**Canmore's
Three Sisters**

*"Hail, King! for so thou art.
Behold,   where   stands
Th'usurper's   cursed   head:
the time is free."*

Macbeth, V, viii

How many other towns can lay claim to being named after a famous king in an even more famous Shakespearean play? Canmore can! Its name was apparently chosen by Donald A. Smith of the Canadian Pacific Railway. It comes from the Gaelic Ceann-mor, meaning 'Big Head' or 'The Large Headed One', a name applied to Malcolm III, King of Scotland from 1057 to 1093. His father was Duncan I, who ruled Scotland from 1034-1040 before being murdered by his brother, Macbeth. Malcolm III was responsible for driving the usurper Macbeth from the throne, defeating him in battle in 1057. He then became king, and ruled until he was killed in battle in 1093.

The Stoney Indians referred to the site occupied by Canmore as *Chuwapchipchiyan Kude Bi*, which literally translates as 'shooting at an animal in the willows'. Legend has it that this either refers to a site at Canmore Flats where young Stoney boys practiced shooting arrows at willow bushes, or where a young brave shot at a burnt stump, thinking it was a wolf. Both are interesting stories. The site was also known as 'Indian Flats' prior to being officially named Canmore. Major Rogers, of Rogers Pass fame, called the spot Padmore, but that name actually applies to a North West Mounted Police station about 18 miles west of Morley near the hamlet of Kananaskis.

Prehistoric Visitors

Archeological evidence indicates that the site of present-day Canmore has been occupied more or less continuously for the past 11,000 years. The Canmore Corridor contains a number of varied prehistoric sites that include stone quarries, campsites, workshops, rock shelters, stone cairns and pictographs. More than thirty prehistoric sites have been investigated in the Canmore Corridor.

The earliest inhabitants from this time period were part of what is known as the Clovis Culture. They were big-game hunters who hunted the large ungulates such as deer, elk and buffalo that frequented the area. The Clovis Culture is known from its distinctive projectile points, which had a groove hollowed out down the middle, allowing for attachment to a shaft.

Other peoples followed the Clovis Culture, each being characterized by distinctive tool assemblages. Finally, around 5,500 BC, the culture of the Mummy Cave Complex spread into the Rocky Mountains. This culture was characterized by small camps in the front ranges, such as the one found at Sibbald Flat. It was eventually replaced by other distinctive cultures until the bow and arrow appeared around 200 AD in association with a culture known as the Avonlea, the probable ancestors of the Kootenay Indians, who spent some time in the Canmore Corridor. The Kootenay were still present in the eastern slopes and foothills when David Thompson passed through in 1800.

Other Native peoples frequented the Canmore Corridor in historic times, but by the early 1840s the Stoney Indians had supplanted the Kootenay and become the dominant culture in the region.

Canmore, the CPR Town

The old town of Canmore is located west of present-day Canmore on the north side of the railway tracks. It is the second-oldest site in the Bow Corridor, after the hamlet of - Kananaskis. Canmore was established in 1884 and was the first divisional point, sixty-eight miles west of Calgary on the railway line. The little depot, a boxcar-like structure, was completed that year, and CPR pioneer Donald A. Smith probably chose the name. Charles Compton was the first station agent, and the first train, engine number 147, rumbling along at a speed of 13 miles an hour, passed through Canmore at noon on May 11, 1884. After this, Canmore became a bustling community.

Canmore and Coal Mining

Part of the growth of Canmore as a community can be attributed to the discovery of coal in the area. An old legend also tells of gold being found on the slopes of Ha Ling Peak. Apparently the first prospectors were successful in extracting about fourteen dollars' worth of gold from a ton of ore. The excavation site is still visible on the lower slopes, but was abandoned as the yield of gold became less.

The Jesuit missionary Father de

Georgetown Collieries, 1917. The office building is to the left and the residence of the Superintendent is to the right.

Smet was the first to report on the mineral resources of the area when he passed through this region on his journey from Oregon in 1845. He noted the abundance of coal outcroppings along the streams in the Canmore Corridor. In 1886 none other than Queen Victoria granted a charter "To mine and extract coal and generally to do all such things as are incidental or conductive to the attainments of the objects aforesaid", in the Canmore area.

In 1884 a promising coal seam was discovered, and led to the formation of the Canmore Coal Company. The first mine was opened in 1887. This company would come to employ nearly 200 men, and had an output of 100 tons of coal per day. Eventually, around 1891, H.W. McNeil acquired control over most of the coal-mining operations in the Bow Valley. By 1908, McNeil provided work for over 300 miners and his mines produced 112,750 tons of coal annually. Canmore Mine Number 2 was opened at this time, which led to the formation of another small mining village east of mineside.

Another new townsite called Georgetown sprang up west of Canmore in 1910. The little village of forty homes was located just outside the present boundary of Banff National Park on the south side of the Bow River. Financial problems due to higher than expected production and shipping costs resulted in the company being placed into receivership in 1916. The mine was closed, but the ugly scar on the side of Mt. Rundle remained for years. Fortunately this site has now been reclaimed.

As long as the demand and price for coal remained high, the mines in the Canmore area remained viable. But as the price for coal dropped and prospective customers dwindled, the end was in sight. With environmental concerns, the mining industry was also presented with a new challenge. Mining in the Canmore area no longer remained viable. The tremendous recent growth of the town of Canmore is due to its becoming a centre for alpine recreational activities.

Sir George Simpson (c. 1790–1860)

Although Sir George Simpson never entered Kananaskis Country, the story of his life was closely intertwined with some of the historical figures who explored this region of the province. He was the governor of the Hudson's Bay Company in North America for almost forty years, and oversaw its vast fur empire in what was then known as Rupert's Land.

Simpson was sent to the Athabasca country in 1820. By 1841 he was governor of Rupert's Land for the Hudson's Bay Company, and one of the most powerful men in the New World — not bad for a man whose formal education probably did not go beyond the parish school in his native Scotland.

Simpson was the illegitimate son of a Scotsman. Who was his mother? When was he born? Where did he go to school? How much education did he receive? As he did his best to erase his beginnings for the records, these questions are without answers, shrouded in the mysterious history of the man who became known as 'The Little Emperor'.

Simpson's abilities as a businessman were more than impressive; he was unquestionably one of the great business leaders of the 19th century. He was intent on developing an active, efficient, and cheap workforce for the company. During his tenure as governor, the value of the company's stock increased enormously, and he made many men wealthy. Through his actions, the North West Company was forced into a merger with the Hudson's Bay Company, and Simpson saw to it that the Hudson's Bay name, holdings, and structure would be paramount. After the merger he streamlined the company and began a series of reforms to reduce costs. He closed many trading posts to eliminate duplication of services, reorganized the administration, and imposed quotas on the trappers. It was easy to dislike the man, but his ruthless tactics would be right at home in many of today's boardrooms.

Simpson's exploits as an explorer were legendary, and he often pushed his men to the limits of their endurance. In 1841, guided by a mixed-blood chief of the Mountain Cree named Piché (or Peechee, as Simpson called him), he became the first European to visit what is now Banff on his way across the mountains to the disputed Oregon Territory.

He was ruthless in his ascent to power, and once achieved, his ego grew enormously and his vanity often influenced his decision-making. Some of the attributes of his character were not very admirable. In fact, many of them could be thought of as repugnant, even for that era.

Simpson: A Flawed Giant of a Man

Was Simpson a racist? By all accounts, the answer is an unequivocal yes. He developed rigid stereotypes about Indians that he expressed throughout most of his life. They were viewed as uncivilized, improvident people who were morally and intellectually retarded. He reserved his harshest comments for the Chippewa, whom he characterized as "cunning, covetous to an extreme, false and cowardly", with a character "disgraceful to human nature." He regarded Indians as "thieving and treacherous", to be treated with contempt.

He displayed an unusual amount of prejudice toward Native women. When his new young wife Frances arrived at the Red River settlement, Simpson seemed determined to create an all-white elite by forbidding the white women to mix with the Native women. The only mixed-blood women who were allowed to come near Mrs. Simpson served her in a purely menial capacity. Simpson even went so far as to rebuff the mixed-blood wives of chief factors in the settlements, rarely allowing them to attend his social functions.

Was Simpson a sexist? Judge for yourself! The governor had a voracious sexual appetite and appeared to be proud of this notorious reputation. He acknowledged seven illegitimate children — two before even reaching North America, and many more were probably scattered across Rupert's Land. Simpson regarded his mixed-blood sexual partners as "his articles" of immediate pleasure, to be disposed of at his convenience. Simpson used a variety of uncomplimentary terms for women of mixed blood, including 'brown jug', 'swarthy idol', and a 'bit of brown'. He completely dominated the life of his beautiful young wife Frances, who bore him five children. Perhaps it was their huge age gap, but George would not allow his wife equal status in their marriage.

Was Simpson egotistical? You be the judge! As his power grew, so did his ego. With an inflated sense of dignity, he increasingly withdrew from his company officers. He attributed this withdrawal as necessary due to their intellectual inferiority and personal limitations. He even hired the services of a piper whose melodies were an impressive addition to Simpson's ceremonial, almost royal, arrival at Hudson's Bay posts. No wonder he became known as the 'Little Emperor' to the officers of the fur trade!

Queen Victoria honoured Simpson with a knighthood in 1841, and with this recognition came Simpson's transition from commercial man to statesman.

Sir George Simpson, in the 1850s

The Kananaskis Valley

Old Bow Fort

left: The Bow River Valley near the "Gap"

right: The remains of Old Bow Fort on the banks of the Bow River

Great things are done when men and mountain meet;
These are not done by scurrying in the street.

William Blake

Stop for a moment at the Morley Flats historical sign, located about one kilometer south of the Trans-Canada junction with Highway 40, and contemplate the history of this valley. Take in the view leading to the Kananaskis Valley. It is the same view observed by James Sinclair in 1841. Not only that; as you travel south into the valley you will be re-tracing human footsteps dating back more than ten thousand years. From its headwaters at the North Kananaskis Pass, the Kananaskis River has cut its valley into the front ranges of the Rocky Mountains to its confluence with the Bow River.

Old Bow Fort (or Peigan Post) was constructed near the junction of the Bow and Kananaskis Rivers in 1832 to facilitate fur trade with the Native people. It was the launching post for many explorations into the mountains. On August 18, 1858, Captain John Palliser left the fort and set off up the valley in search of the legendary Kananaskis Pass. Shortly after leaving the post, he saw the valley for the first time near present-day Barrier Lake, and wrote in his journal, "A magnificent view of its valley, hemmed in on either side by an unbroken wall of mountains, the sides of which for 1,000 feet were richly clad in pine."

Considerable geological turbulence was involved in the formation of the middle and upper parts of the Kananaskis Valley. The entire valley runs from Barrier Lookout south to the Kananaskis Lakes and is entirely within the front ranges. Over 120 million years ago, major thrust faults and folds produced a series of narrow, linear mountain ranges, including the Opal Range on the east side of the valley and the Kananaskis Range on the west. For the most part, these mountains are composed of limestones, sandstones, and shales ranging in age from 550 million to 136 million years. The oldest rocks in Kananaskis Country, 550-million-year-old limestones, are found on the northwest side of Barrier Lake near the bottom of Barrier Lookout.

The Kananaskis Valley from Kananaskis Trail

Prehistory of the Valley

The Mummy Cave Complex

About 8,000 to 10,000 years ago, long before the first Europeans viewed these mountains, the prehistoric people of the Mummy Cave complex roamed the valleys of Kananaskis. They left evidence of their passing in the form of tools, bone fragments, and broken bits of pottery and art. This group of hunter-gatherers is named after a cave in northwest Wyoming where they left artifacts. It is possible that they occupied the cave at the Upper Grassi Lake, where pictographs can be seen on rock surfaces. They also left new varieties of side-notched projectile points, which allowed them to attach the points to wooden shafts in a new and innovative manner.

Major campsites and work sites where hunters prepared their weapons and butchered their game were unearthed during construction of the Kananaskis Trail (Highway 40) in the early 1970s. Over 150 archeological sites with artifacts have been identified in Kananaskis Country. One such site was discovered in the Wasootch Creek area near Wasootch Tower. Perhaps this unique tower served as a landmark for these nomads as they wandered through the valley on their seasonal migrations. The name Wasootch was derived from the Stoney name *Wasiju Waptan,* which means 'White Man Creek'. Visitors to any of these sites should be careful not to disrupt, destroy, or even touch any of the artifacts, as they are extremely fragile.

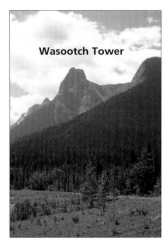

Wasootch Tower from Wasootch Creek on the Kananaskis Trail

Archeological evidence unearthed from sites in the Kananaskis Valley seems to indicate that these sites were base camps used on a seasonal basis for thousands of years. These first humans in the region hunted bison, elk, deer, moose, mountain sheep and goats, using spears tipped with projectile points chipped out of locally available siliceous siltstone. Meat-scraping tools, stone knives, and chipping stones have been excavated from these sites. Strong evidence also suggests that plants were harvested for food as well as for medicinal and ceremonial functions.

The Mummy Cave complex was followed by two major cultures that also left evidence of their habitation in the Kananaskis region. The first was the Pelican Lake culture, which made tools from exotic rocks such as obsidian, and introduced buffalo jumps as a hunting strategy. They also left their signature in the form of teepee rings that first appeared sometime after 5,500 BC. The Pelican Lake culture was supplanted by the Besant culture, which is credited with adding buffalo pounds to hunting strategy. In this form of hunt, the buffalo were driven into containing compounds, where they could then be slaughtered. The Besant culture is also credited with introducing the first bow and arrow for hunting and with pioneering the first use of pottery by prehistoric cultures between AD 200 and 1700.

Prehistoric Technology

The prehistoric people of Alberta used a variety of raw materials to make tools for hunting, scraping hides, and preparing their food. Some of these tools, particularly those made of stone, have survived for thousands of years and are common artifacts found in archeological sites. Stone tools were made from local rock using techniques called percussion flaking and pressure flaking, and these tools, along with waste materials from their manufacture, are found at the sites.

The Use of Medicinal Plants

It is not known exactly how prehistoric people learned of the medicinal properties or the food value of many mountain plants. Perhaps this information was discovered by simple trial and error and then passed down from generation to generation by word of mouth. Two common plants that found their way into medicine bags were willow *(Salix sp.)* and yarrow *(Achillea millefolium)*.

They also somehow found that chewing the inner bark of willow would alleviate all types of aches and pains. Today we know that this analgesic property comes from a chemical in these plants called salicin, which has effects similar to those of Aspirin. They also determined that willow leaves had an astringent quality that was very effective when placed on cuts or wounds.

The common yarrow plant had all sorts of medicinal uses. It was used as a tonic to relieve colds and fevers, and perhaps its most important use was its ability to stop bleeding. Leaves tied to a wound would effectively stop the bleeding fairly quickly and aid the healing process.

The Assiniboine Indians: People Who Cook With Stones

By the time Europeans arrived in southern Alberta, what is now known as the Kananaskis Valley had been used for centuries by many Native tribes, including the Kootenay, Salish, and Snake Indians. A series of displacements occurred, and dominant tribes succeeded one another. In other cases, such as occurred in 1780, the Salish and Kootenay were decimated by smallpox.

The Stoney Indians eventually attained a permanent foothold on the eastern slopes. Their name was not derived from the fact that they inhabited the eastern slopes of the Rocky Mountains, but rather from their method of cooking. Before pots and kettles were introduced by Europeans, the Stoneys would dig holes in the ground and line them with wet rawhide. Into these rawhide bowls they put pieces of meat along with wild vegetables, which they then cooked by dropping very hot rocks into the bowls.

Although Mt. Assiniboine does not lie within Kananaskis Country, it is included here because of its historical connection to the Stoney Nation, and because everyone wants to see the 'Matterhorn of the Rockies'. George Dawson named the peak in 1885 in honour of the Assiniboine Indians, who have been part of the history of this region for hundreds of years. Father Pierre-Jean de Smet was probably the first European to view this majestic pyramid when he passed through the Spray River valley in 1845 on his way across the Great Divide from Oregon. In 1901, James Outram and Swiss guides Christian Hasler and C. Bohren were the first to attain the summit of Mount Assiniboine.

The Legend of the Yahey Wichastabi

The Stoney were an offshoot of the Plains Assiniboine, from whom they separated in the early 1600s. Seeking a new homeland, they braved great dangers in migrating westward to the Rocky Mountains. They were led by Nakoda and White Light — spirit men who received their powers from *Waka taga*. The lodges that followed the spirit men west called themselves *Yahey Wichastabi* ('Mountain People'). Somewhere in the Dakotas, Nakoda made his great death song and was carried into the sky by the Great White Eagle. White Light led the people the rest of the way to the land they had dreamed of, the *Yahey Yamnaska*, where they live to this day. Life in the mountains changed the lifestyle of the Stoney, but their sheltered environment in the mountains also protected them from the dreaded smallpox.

The Stoney were generally a peaceful people, but were also respected as fierce warriors. They preferred the isolation and solitude afforded by the Bow and Kananaskis valleys, and because of this, managed to avoid most of the wars and epidemics that regularly swept across the Great Plains. Today, ancestors of these great people still inhabit the

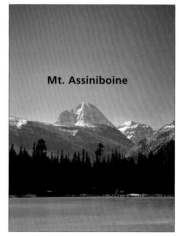

Mt. Assiniboine

The only location for viewing Mount Assiniboine from a major roadway in Kananaskis Country is at Buller Pond, on the Smith-Dorrien/Spray Trail, 28 km north of the junction with the Kananaskis Lakes Trail.

area centered on the village of Morley, near the junction of the Bow and Kananaskis rivers.

The Legend of Nakoda: The First Stoney Man

Iktomni, the eldest brother of *Waka taga*, is sitting on a rainbow and arrives on earth to find the animal people arguing among themselves. At a place of clay he takes up some earth and mixes the soil with clay and dust and water and makes it into the shape of a man. He places the clay under the Great Star. When the star heat dries the man out, he summons the Four Winds to blow life into the clay man. After south wind blows life into the man, he sees that he has placed the man too close to the Great Star and that he is burnt. This is the origin of the black man. He makes another man. East wind breathes life into the clay, but the man is too far from the great star and is pale. This is the origin of the yellow man. The third man is set even farther away. North wind blows life into the clay man who becomes the first white man. *Iktomni* builds a fourth man. The west wind blows life into his nostrils. This one is tan and just right. *Iktomni* says, "I name you Nakoda, First Stoney Man. You are the fourth. And because Great Star dries you out evenly on this flat boulder, you will be called Stoney. *Waka taga* chooses you as a special nation, a nation that will one day bring together all their dark, yellow and white brothers. They are to watch over all living creatures and not to neglect them."

The Palliser Expedition (1857–1860)

By the mid-nineteenth century, the British government had become alarmed at American exploration into western North America, which included plans to link with the Pacific by railway. Not much was known about the British territories west of the Red River. Even less was known of the Rocky Mountain barrier and the passes that existed across it.

In 1857 the British government, on the recommendation of the Royal Geographical Society, agreed to sponsor Captain John Palliser, a 42-year-old Irishman, to lead an expedition to North America. There, scientific data was to be collected on the climate, geology, geography, flora and fauna, and potential for agriculture of the relatively unexplored western regions. Palliser was instructed to investigate the land and collect the data from the area between Lake Superior and the Red River, the area between the Red River west to the Rocky Mountains between the 49th parallel and the North Saskatchewan River, as well as the Rocky Mountains themselves and the possible routes across them.

Palliser was awarded 5000 pounds from the government treasury to cover expenses. His expedition took place between 1857 and 1860.

George Simpson happened to be in England in 1856, and in meeting Palliser gave him valuable information and advice and even arranged for Hudson's Bay Company supplies to be at Palliser's disposal when he reached North America. In addition, Palliser had met James Sinclair in 1848, and Sinclair had already crossed the Great Divide by a pass south of that used by Simpson in 1841. Sinclair had described this pass to Palliser, who immediately became interested in seeing it for himself.

What type of man was Palliser? He was described by his guide and interpreter Peter Erasmus as being "quite tall, and always appeared to hold himself erect so that he had a straight-backed military appearance." His voice was described as pleasantly smooth, and he expressed each word with exact and clear pronunciation. All the men who accompanied Palliser respected his authority, not because of his rank, but because he was sincerely concerned for their welfare. As Erasmus told it, "The character of the man himself and his attitude of friendly equality aroused a loyalty that was greater than mere respect. Every man was stirred to give his best to any task assigned to him." Palliser was also deeply religious and forbade any exploratory work on Sunday.

Joining Palliser were Dr. James Hector, a 21-year-old Scot who held degrees in medicine and geology; Eugène Bourgeau, a botanist in charge of making an inventory of the flora of the region; and Lieutenant Thomas Blakiston, who would survey Rupert's Land to supplement the maps of David Thompson and Peter Fidler.

John William Sullivan was appointed the expedition's astronomer and secretary. Peter Erasmus, as mentioned, served as the party's guide and interpreter.

Intrigue: A Mission for the British Secret Service?

The Treaty of Ghent, signed in 1818, had officially brought to a close the war of 1812 between England and the United States. It also established the 49th parallel as the international border as far west as the eastern slopes of the Rocky Mountains. Settlement of the Oregon Dispute in 1846 extended the boundary along the 49th parallel west over the mountains to thePacific Ocean.

Captain John Palliser

Some evidence exists that the Palliser Expedition was carrying out, in part, a mission for the newly-formed British Secret Service. Both Captain John Palliser and the first head of the Secret Service, Lieutenant-Colonel Thomas Best Jervis, were members of the Royal Geographical Society, which provided Palliser with support for this expedition. Palliser's primary object was to provide detailed maps of western North America, and these maps were one of the Secret Service's most coveted prizes. In fact, at the time of the Palliser Expedition, the British Secret Service was known as the "Topographical and Statistical Department", and maps were its fundamental reason for existence.

Palliser's maps served as the primary geographical source of information used by the North West Mounted Police in 1874, when they set forth to occupy what was then called the 'North-West Territories' of Canada. It also appears that Palliser was carrying out an analysis of the most sensible route for a transcontinental railroad that would solidify Canada's claim to these western territories, which were also coveted by the United States.

Rediscovery & Naming of Kananaskis Pass

In his journal entry for August 18, 1858, Palliser wrote, "At noon we had completed the preparations for our departure and, with a party of four men and nine horses, commenced our journey across the Rocky Moun-

Fall splendour along the Kananaskis River

tains. Ascending the Bow River for about five miles, we forded the stream at the distance of about half a mile above where the Kananaskis River joins it."

If this journal entry describes the scene accurately, then Palliser actually began his search for the legendary pass described by James Sinclair by entering the ravine at present-day Quaite Creek. From here, the group would have entered Kananaskis Valley by going over Jewel Pass and emerging on the north side of present-day Barrier Lake. Following old Native trails on the west bank of the Kananaskis River, they reached present-day Boundary Flats on August

20, 1858.

Palliser named the pass he sought "Kananaskis", after the legend of an Indian of that name who had made a "most wonderful recovery from the blow of an axe, which had stunned him but had failed to kill him." Rumour has it that the Indian received the blow to the head somewhere near the present-day Kananaskis ranger station near Palliser's camping spot of August 20, 1858. Today the pass, valley, river, and a range of mountains bear this name.

The Stoney had many other names for the Kananaskis River. *Ozade Imne Wapta,* or more simply *Ozade,* referred to the Y-shaped fork in the river between the Kananaskis and Bow Rivers. The most interesting name is *Nikeichichiyabi Mini,* which stems from an ancient legend that the pure, clean waters of the river were spiritual and life-giving.

When Palliser reached the Upper Kananaskis Lake he was stunned by its beauty. He describes coming to a "magnificent lake, hemmed in by mountains, and studded by numerous islets, very thickly wooded." He was only the second known European to view the 40-foot waterfall between the Upper and Lower Kananaskis Lakes. The Native name for the Upper Kananaskis Lake was *Ozade Imne* or 'Lake at the forks'. Their name for the Lower Kananaskis Lake was *Ozade Imne ima ze* or 'The other lake at the forks'.

Palliser's party continued past Lawson Lake and proceeded to Maude Lake at the summit of North Kananaskis Pass (2363 m), arriving at the pass on August 22, just 5 days after leaving Old Bow Fort. South Kananaskis Pass was called *Iya anibi,* or 'Climb mountain pass', because of the scrambling required to attain its summit. Palliser does not appear to have known of that pass, as he makes no mention of it in his report or journal. Maude Lake was called *Iyarhe*

Apadaha Iyabize or 'Lake by the pass', referring to Kananaskis Pass.

Palliser descended to a river west of the pass, which now bears his name, and later returned to Fort Edmonton via the Kootenay Pass. Although he thought that a road over the pass to the Columbia River would not be a very "arduous undertaking", his secretary later discouraged him from considering this route. James Hector's route over Kicking Horse Pass became the route into the future.

So Captain John Palliser became only the second person of European descent to view the wonders of the Kananaskis Valley. No monument to either him or James Sinclair, however, is to be found in Kananaskis Country, honouring either man or event!

An Alarming Controversy: Did Palliser Really Cross Kananaskis Pass?

There are a growing number who do not think that Palliser crossed North Kananaskis Pass. Larry Boyd (1999) continues to gather evidence to prove that Elk Pass is the real Kananaskis Pass named and crossed by Palliser in 1858. Unfortunately, Palliser's personal papers were lost in a fire and historians have had to rely on *The Papers of the Palliser Expedition*, edited by Irene Spry and published by the Champlain Society, as the accepted authority on the Palliser Expedition.

Camping at a spot about four miles south of Boundary Flats near Grizzly or Hood Creek, Palliser describes sighting two very conspicuous mountains about twelve miles south of his encampment. This was the height of land Palliser said his group would have to cross to gain the west-

ern side of the watershed, stating, "This pass I have called Kananaskis Pass." The only two prominent mountains that can be seen to the south of this viewpoint are Mount Fox and Mount Aosta, and they frame Elk Pass. Was it Elk Pass that was identified by Palliser as the real Kananaskis Pass? Many now consider this to be the case. To further complicate matters, Palliser states in a report to Lord Stanley in October 1858, "I am rejoiced to say that I have completely succeeded in discovering not only a pass practicable for horses, but one which, with but little expense, could be rendered available for carts also." For those of us who have hiked across North and South Kananaskis passes, it would seem neither could be the pass Palliser is talking about.

On August 22, 1858, Palliser reached the height of land and camped at a small lake (presumably Maude Lake), from which "flow the first waters we had seen which descend to the Pacific Ocean." It is commonly known that the outlet waters of Maude Lake at North Kananaskis Pass flow east, and not towards the western watershed. Irene Spry suggests that an avalanche has since blocked the western outlet since Palliser's 1858 visit. Either Palliser had his directions all wrong, or Elk Pass is the pass that Palliser named Kananaskis Pass.

The plot thickens with more confusing evidence. Barometric pressure readings by Palliser gave a calculated elevation of the pass he crossed as 5,985 feet. The elevation of North Kananaskis Pass is 7,800 feet, while that of Elk Pass is 6,000 feet. Allowing for variations in barometric pressure to result in a maximum error of 200 feet, something is drastically wrong with these measurements. Either Palliser is wrong in his calculations, or Elk Pass is the actual Kananaskis Pass named by Palliser, and the history books must be rewritten!

The Legend of the Indian Paintbrush

This is probably the most recognizable and favourite plant in the Canadian Rockies, but it is a taxonomist's nightmare. There are at least six and possibly ten species of the plant to be found in the mountains. *Castilleja miniatum* is the scientific name of the common red variety. There are many other varieties of this plant, ranging in colour from magenta to yellow to almost white, but you might have to hike into the alpine meadows in order to observe some of these.

Indian paintbrush

What most people do not know is that this plant is semi-parasitic on the roots of other plants. And to confuse matters even more, the flowers aren't even flower petals, but colourful floral bracts. The actual petals are tiny inconspicuous flowers found inside these bracts.

An Old Indian Legend

In the days before the white man came, a Blackfoot maiden fell in love with a wounded prisoner she was attending. She realized that the tribe was only nursing its captive in order to torture and sacrifice him later. She planned an escape for the prisoner in which she would accompany him to escape being punished herself for such a deed. In the middle of the night the two made their successful escape.

After some time in her lover's camp, the maiden grew homesick for a glimpse of her old camp. She finally went to visit it, and while hiding in the bushes, overheard young braves discussing the punishment that was to be her due for her traitorous action, if they could only find her. The maiden realized that she could never return to her home, so decided to take back with her a drawing of her old camp. Cutting a gash in her foot, she dipped a twig in the blood and drew a picture of the camp on a piece of bark. After completing the picture, she threw the stick away and returned to her adopted home. Where the twig fell, there grew a little plant with a brush-like end, dyed with the blood of the maiden. This plant became the first Indian Paintbrush.

Who Was Peter Erasmus?

Peter Erasmus (1833–1931) was a colourful character who looms large in the history of western Canada. Highly educated and fluent in many languages, Erasmus was the perfect choice to serve as guide and interpreter for the Palliser Expedition.

It is fascinating to read the history of western Canada. Some of us wish we had been part of it. Few ever get the chance to play a role in the making of history, but Peter Erasmus not only experienced the formation of western Canada, he also played an active part in its development. As a member of the Palliser Expedition, he is one of but a few men to have known these explorers personally and to have written about their travels. His impressions and observations of the character and attitudes of these gentlemen are one of the few first-hand accounts left for historians.

Peter Erasmus was born in 1833 to a Danish father and an Ojibwa mixed-blood mother. His father had fought at Waterloo before becoming an employee of the Hudson's Bay Company. Peter was highly educated and had been trained by Reverend Woolsey for Methodist missionary work. He became fluent in six Native languages as well as Latin and Greek. Much respected by the Native peoples, settlers, and explorers, he was the major interpreter at the signing of Treaty No. 6.

George Gooderham of the Alberta Historical Review met Erasmus in 1909 when he was 76 years old, and described him as a big man with a scruffy beard. But his most prominent facial feature was his nose, described as "a mass of pitted flesh that laid flat across his brown face." This cancerous growth had apparently been caused by a bruise in a trail ride accident and been further irritated by frequent freezing. It was Dr. Hector who had the opportunity to use some ancient Stoney medicine and natural healing to bring a halt to its growth.

Erasmus was eyewitness to the Riel Rebellion of 1885. He also helped negotiate one of the treaties by which the Plains Indians gave up their tribal lands to the Crown, and he worked tirelessly to get them settled on reserves. Sadly, he also witnessed the disappearance of the buffalo.

Peter Erasmus

Peter Erasmus, trapper, hunter, interpreter, guide, explorer, and trader died in 1931 at the age of ninety-seven at Whitefish Lake, Montana. His unmarked grave sits on a hill overlooking the lake. In honour of his exploits, the Geographic Board of Canada in 1930 made Mount Erasmus an official peak in the Canadian Rockies.

Gateway To the Kananaskis Valley

Mt. Baldy

Mount Baldy from Kananaskis Trail, just past the entrance to Kananaskis Country

Barrier Lookout 1996 m

For many generations, the Stoney Indians used Barrier Mountain as a lookout. Referring to their traditional enemy, the Blackfoot, they called it *Tokyapebi ipa*, meaning 'a lookout point for the enemy'. The approach of hostile war parties across the plains could be seen from a long way, much like the extensive views the lookout offers today for entirely different purposes. At other times the Stoney simply called the lookout *Iyarhe ipa* ('Mountain cliff'), which aptly describes the shape of the northeast end of Barrier Mountain. The oldest known rocks in the Kananaskis Valley, 550-million-year-old Cambrian carbonates, occur in the cliffs on the northwest side of Barrier Lake.

Today, Barrier Mountain serves as a fire lookout. If you look carefully, the tower can be seen on the summit. The original lookout on McConnell Ridge was one of the guard towers at POW Camp #130 during World War II. It was nicknamed Pigeon Lookout after the stool pigeons who manned the tower during the war. It was replaced in 1984 with a new, fully modern shelter that is supplied by helicopter on top of Barrier Mountain.

The prisoners of war from Camp #130 were instrumental in the construction of Barrier Lake, which would create a reservoir for the production of hydroelectric power. In order not to breach the terms of the Geneva Convention outlining the handling of prisoners, only those prisoners who volunteered were enlisted for this work. They were paid $3.50 per day to clear timber from the land that was to become Barrier Lake. When water levels are low, stumps from this clearing project can still be seen. Subsequent construction of the dam on the Kananaskis River by Calgary Power flooded 673 acres of cleared forest.

Mount Baldy 2192 m

The Stoney called Mt. Baldy 'Sleeping Buffalo Mountain' long before it received its present name. If you use your imagination, you may be able to discern the hump and shape of a buffalo in the outline of the mountain as you drive south on the Kananaskis Trail. The German POWs were allowed to climb the mountain for exercise if they promised not to try to escape. After a new snowfall, they thought the peak resembled a bald head. This was not the first time it had been called by this name. Kendall Kerr of the Eau Claire Logging Company had suggested the name 'Bald Mountain' as early as 1883. The name 'Barrier Mountain' became popular after 1945 because the mountain overlooks Barrier Lake, but in 1984 Mt. Baldy was finally made the official name.

Mount McDougall
2726 m

Mount McDougall is a large, rather nondescript mountain, with many minor summits. It was named in honour of the Rev. George McDougall, a Methodist missionary. He arrived at Fort Edmonton in 1862 with his wife, two daughters and two sons. They established a mission close to Fort Edmonton, where they worked ceaselessly with the Cree Indians.

The mountain is nothing more than a stiff scramble, and was first ascended in 1952, with no difficulties, by a large party from the Alpine Club of Canada. A fairly good viewpoint for the mountain is from the vicinity of Wedge Pond on the Kananaskis Trail. If you look eastward from this vantage point, both Mt. McDougall and Old Baldy dominate the skyline.

The McDougall family was a firsthand witness to the scourges of the smallpox epidemic that swept the plains in the early 1870s, losing both daughters to the disease. Rev. McDougall's two sons, John and David,

Mt. McDougall · **Old Baldy**

established the mission near Morley in 1873 in a temporary birchbark structure, which was later replaced by the Morley Memorial Church. They also built a new schoolhouse, and in 1875 they brought Andrew Sibbald from Ontario to be its headmaster. The McDougall family was also the first to bring a head of twelve cattle from Edmonton to Morley, where they grazed. The brand 'JM' was used for John's cattle, and 'O' for David's.

Tragedy struck the McDougall family again in the nasty winter of 1876. Food supplies were running low when word came that a herd of buffalo had been spotted within a day's travel of Morley. George, his son John, a cousin from Ontario, and two Stoney Indians made up a hunting party, and they went after the buffalo in the deep prairie snow. Six animals were slaughtered, skinned, and quartered, and the meat was loaded onto sleighs. George announced that he would ride ahead and cook supper for the party at the camp.

When John and the others arrived at the camp, George was nowhere to be found. A search was unsuccessful, so the hunting party started for home, assuming that the elder missionary had simply gone on to Morley without them. But the elder McDougall was not there either. After many days of searching, his horse was found, and finally the frozen body of

Reverend George McDougall

Mt. McDougall and Old Baldy from the helipad at Kananaskis Village

Fisher Peak

A magnificent view of Fisher Peak from the Kananaskis Trail at the bridge over Evan-Thomas Creek, 4.6 km south of the junction to Nakiska ski area

Reverend George was found too, with his arms folded across his chest. He was buried near what is now Hwy. 1A just outside Morley. His last letter had been a request that an orphanage be built on the reserve, and this wish was granted in 1879.

Old Baldy 2382 m

This insignificant summit just poking its head above treeline can be seen on the east side of the Kananaskis Trail almost anywhere in the vicinity of Kananaskis Village. It is best viewed after the first snowfall and throughout the winter, when the origin of its name becomes obvious!

Fisher Peak 3053 m

Fisher Peak is found in the Fisher Range, approximately 8 km southeast of The Wedge. The peak was named in honour of John Arbuthnot ('Jackie') Fisher (1841-1920). Fisher was one of seven children born to a coffee planter in Ceylon, whose position was so wretched that he had to ship his children back to England to live off the charity of his relatives.

'Jackie' Fisher

Jackie Fisher joined the Royal Navy at the age of 13, penniless, friendless, and forlorn. He worked diligently and soon learned seamanship and mathematics. At the age of 20 he turned to gunnery, learning all the new techniques and soon becoming an instructor. He became captain of the *Inflexible* at the age of 33 and was involved in the bombardment of Alexandria in 1882. Upon returning to England he became the Director of Naval Ordinance, Admiral Superintendent of Portsmouth Dockyard, and was finally promoted to First Sea Lord on Oct. 21, 1904—a post he held until his resignation in 1910.

Jackie Fisher was responsible for modernizing and overseeing the transformation of the antiquated Victorian British Navy into a 20th century fighting fleet. He was outspoken, iconoclastic, and technically minded. His sweeping aside of traditional attitudes and naval design aroused the antagonism of many of his colleagues. Larger firepower and speed were his motto in a design revolution that produced a grand British naval fleet. As First Sea Lord he oversaw new ship design that led to the development of the first dreadnought battleship, as well as new battle cruisers and destroyers. He also championed the development of submarines for the Royal Fleet. When he retired in 1910 at the age of 69, his Grand Fleet, as it was known, was ready to rule the seas.

During the First World War, after the sacking of First Sea Lord Prince Louis of Battenberg on October 29, 1914, Fisher once again resumed the role of First Sea Lord until May 15, 1915, when he resigned over the campaign in the Dardanelles.

When he was knighted, Sir Jackie Fisher chose as his motto 'Fear God and Dread Nought'.

Mount Lorette 2484 m

Mount Lorette was named after Lorette Spur, a minor high point to the north of Vimy Ridge that was captured by the French army during World War I. It is unclear why this spur warranted having a mountain named after it, since it was Vimy Ridge itself that proved to be Canada's greatest achievement of World War I.

The Stoney Indians called the mountain *Kiska tha wakoneya Zen Iyarhe ze* ('the mountain by goat springs'). If you plan on picnicking around the Lorette Ponds to enjoy the views, you should know that this is where the Stoney used to trap beaver. They called the ponds *Chabti oda naze* ('Many beaver lodges').

In May 1952, R.C. Hind, B. Richardson, I. Keeling, J. Manry, J. Dodds, and C. McAllister made the first ascent of the mountain via its south ridge. In June 1966, H. Gude and G. Crocker performed the first traverse — a feat of extraordinary endurance. The two climbed the south ridge and proceeded to traverse northwest over an unnamed 2661-metre summit, an unnamed 2750-metre summit, and finally over Mt. McGillivray, reaching the Trans-Canada Highway in thirteen hours!

Vimy Ridge: Canada's Greatest Achievement of World War I

"I looked ahead and saw the German front line crashing into pieces; bits of men, timbers, and lumps of chalk were flying through the air, and blending with the shattering wall of fire. We didn't dare lift our heads, knowing that the barrage was to come flat over us and then lift in three minutes. That queer empty stomach feeling had gone. I don't think anyone was scared. Instead one's whole body seemed to be in a mad macabre dance."

Gus Sivertz, 3rd Canadian Division on Vimy Ridge

Vimy Ridge, a 60-metre high ridge captured by the Germans in October 1914, became a strategic, seemingly invincible high point that controlled the surrounding countryside. Both the French and British had made unsuccessful attempts to capture the ridge. The French alone suffered over 150,000 casualties between May and November 1915. By the end of May 1917, the British would also suffer over 71,000 casualties. Vimy Ridge had become a killing field.

On the evening of April 8, 1917, 30,000 soldiers of the Canadian Corps began to move to the front line. At 5:30 the next morning, Easter Monday, the Canadian infantry went over the top into no man's land. The Currie Division captured the Zwolfer Graben trench system within thirty minutes, while Major-General L.J. Lipsett and the 3rd Division captured the huge Schwaben tunnel system.

By April 12, four days later, the Canadians were firmly in control of Vimy Ridge, capturing 124 German machine guns and taking over 4,000 prisoners. Unfortunately the battle was not won without a heavy toll. The Canadian Corps suffered 3,598 casualties, and another 7,004 men were wounded.

It is hard to describe or imagine the horrors the soldiers of the Canadian Corps must have seen, or what they felt. Destruction and death was everywhere. George Frederick Murray, a young private from New Brunswick in the 5th Canadian Mounted Rifles, relates that the entire slope had become a shambles:

"Every foot of ground was churned up; thousands of gaping shell holes were slowly filling with bloody water, arms, legs, and other pieces of

Mt. Lorette

Mount Lorette from Lorette Ponds day use area on the Kananaskis Trail, 18.7 km from the junction with the Trans-Canada Highway

dismembered bodies; and equipment of both sides was strewn about like garbage— abandoned rifles, steel helmets, bits of flesh, all bound together with a mucilage of mud."

The capture of Vimy Ridge was a matter of national pride for our young independent nation. These men of the Canadian Corps represented many cultures from across Canada, and most had enlisted as untrained volunteers. After the success at Vimy, the Canadian Corps became one of the most skilled and respected fighting battalions of World War I.

Peaks of the Opal Range

The peaks of the Opal Range had their origins in the sediments laid down in ancient seas of Devonian times some 300 million years ago. Typical life forms found in these ancient seas were the first plants, placoderm fish, brachiopods, and solitary and colonial corals. The exposed limestone outcroppings of these mountains contain a multitude of fossil corals.

Opal Ridge

In 1884, geologist Dr. George Dawson mistakenly named these spectacularly eroded limestone peaks for "the jointed surfaces coated with films of opal" he thought the rock contained. Subsequent investigation has revealed no opal deposits, but rather a look-alike chert composed of silica imbedded with various quartz impurities. The spectacular shape of the range is due to vertical dipping beds of limestone rock of the Rundle Group that have been eroded into spectacular pinnacles over the millennia. There are

King Creek Ridge

many names for peaks eroded in this fashion, including ripsaw, dogtooth, and flatirons. These eroded pinnacles are ancient, ranging in age from 230 to 300 million years old.

Peaks of the Opal Range are difficult to view from the Kananaskis Trail due to the intervening Opal and King Creek ridges. They are spectacular from higher elevations if you can hike to them, but fortunately there are also three good sites on accessible roadways from which to view the range: the access road to Fortress Mountain ski area, the Peninsula day use area on the Smith-Dorrien/Spray Trail, and the north end of the Interlakes parking lot on the Kananaskis Lakes Trail.

Opal Ridge (2597 m) and King Creek Ridge (2423 m)

Opal Ridge is an 8-kilometre-long ridge on the east (left) side of the Kananaskis Valley as you travel south on the Kananaskis Trail. It extends from Rocky Creek at the north end to Grizzly Creek at the south. This is one of the most spectacular ridges from which to view the entire length of the

Opal Range to the east and the Kananaskis Range to the west, separated far below by the Kananaskis Valley. Every weekend the ridge is popular with scramblers anxious for spectacular views and willing to challenge its muscle-aching 1000 vertical meters.

King Creek Ridge commemorates William Henry 'Willie' King (1875-1941), a rancher in the Millarville area and coal prospector with George Pocaterra. The Stoney Indians knew the ridge by the name *Kiska tha Iyarhe* ('Goat Mountain'), obviously referring to the animal they hunted on the ridge long ago. This is another of those 'must-do' ridges from which to obtain glorious views of the peaks of the Opal Range immediately east, and Mt. Wintour and the Kananaskis Lakes to the west. However, in order to obtain these sights, you will have to expend some energy to reach the summit of the ridge.

The Wedge 2665 m

'The Wedge' is a descriptive name that refers to the distinctive shape of the peak's wedge-like double summit. No information is available on its first ascent. The north and south summits are separated by a narrow ridge that must be crossed *'au cheval'* (straddling the sharp edge) in order to attain the main summit. Ben Gadd and R. Ballard were first to ascend the north face, which is seen in the photo, in July 1970.

Wedge Pond, a favorite day use area, was once known to the Stoney as *Chapta Mne* (Pine Lake) because of the few trees that once circled the lake. It was also a favourite camping spot for the Kootenay Indians when they crossed the Great Divide to hunt in the Kananaskis Valley.

Although there has always been a freshwater pond here, it was enlarged by almost a hectare to a depth of 12 metres during the construction of the

Panorama of The Wedge and adjacent mountains

Kananaskis Country Golf Course. Two hundred thousand cubic meters of soil were removed in 33,000 truckloads to create the lush fairways of the golf course.

Mackay Hills (high point 2454 m) were named after Walter Grant Mackay, a turn-of-the-century prospector, who set a claim after discovering coal in the area.

Mount Denny 3000 m

Mount Denny is a spectacular double-peaked mountain. Until 1973, the centennial year of the Royal Canadian Mounted Police, it had remained unnamed. Unless you hike to the top of a ridge, only the top of this mountain can be viewed from a major roadway.

The south peak was first ascended in March 1973, solo, by J. Martin via the southwest face. In July 1973, D. Forest, G. Boles, and M. Simpson climbed the south peak, recording the second ascent, and then continued to traverse the mountain to the north peak, which was climbed for the first time in what Glen Boles called a "very enjoyable scramble."

The double summits of Mount Denny from Opal Ridge

59

Mt. Potts

Mt. Evan-Thomas

Mt. Packenham

Panorama of Mt. Potts and Mt. Evan-Thomas from the summit of Opal Ridge

These three then submitted the name of Sir Cecil Edward Denny (1855-1928) to the naming commission, and the name became official that same year.

The Story of Cecil Denny

Cecil Denny was born in England into a minister's family. At 19, he immigrated to the United States and found his way to Canada in 1874 as a captain in the North West Mounted Police. After an arduous trek west, he aided Colonel Macleod in the building of Fort Macleod in the winter of 1874-75, and then in August of 1875 was in charge of the detachment that built Fort Calgary.

In 1882, after eight years, Denny resigned from the Mounted Police to become the Indian Agent to the Cree, Assiniboine and Blackfoot. These Indian nations made Denny an honourary chief, bestowing on him the title 'Chief Beaver Coat', owing to his favourite overcoat made from beaver fur. Later, in 1885, Denny established the ranch he had dreamed of near Fort Macleod.

When the Northwest Rebellion broke out in 1885, Denny was asked by the government of Sir John A.

Captain Cecil Denny

Macdonald to be special Indian Agent charged with helping to maintain the peace with the Indians of southern Alberta, in order to dissuade them from joining the uprising taking place in Saskatchewan.

After his death in 1928, Denny was accorded a full public funeral in Calgary and buried in the Mounted Police plot in the city he helped establish.

Mount Potts 3000 m

Mount Potts was named in honour of Jerry Potts, legendary scout of the North West Mounted Police.

There is some confusion regarding the first ascent of this peak. The first ascent occurred in July 1954, by Miss J. Farman, M.S. Hicks, W. Lemmon, G. Ross, Miss I. Spreat, and J.F. Tarrant, who mistakenly thought they had climbed Mt. Evan-Thomas. In 1954, on the very same day Tarrant's party thought they were on Evan-Thomas, they were viewed by another party led by S. Pearson from what they thought was Mt. Packenham. Mt. Potts is not visible from Mt. Packenham. Pearson's party must therefore have been on Mt. Evan-Thomas and Tarrant's party on Mt. Potts. This was all made apparent in 1973, when a party led by Glen Boles discovered a copper canister in a summit cairn after completing what they assumed was the first ascent of Mt. Potts. (Whew—glad we got all that straightened out!)

The Legend of Jerry Potts

Jerry Potts was born in about 1840 to a Blood Indian mother named Namopisi (Crooked Back) and a Scotsman named Andrew R. Potts. Jerry's life became one of violence and tragedy. Anything but handsome, Jerry Potts was of small stature with rounded shoulders, bow-legged, and pigeon-toed. While still a baby, a Peigan Indian mistakenly killed his father and Jerry was adopted by Alexander Harvey, one of the most notorious characters of the Upper Missouri region. When Harvey was forced to leave the frontier due to his lawless exploits, the young Jerry was abandoned at the tender age of five.

Andrew Dawson, a gentle Scotsman, then adopted him. Under his patient guidance the young Potts learned English, Indian languages, and the ways of both the Indian and the white man. By the time he had reached his teens he was renowned as a guide and had become a crack marksman with both rifle and revolver. He had an uncanny ability to remember every detail and landmark of the frontier, even in storm or darkness.

Potts was engaged by the North West Mounted Police in 1874 as a scout and interpreter, a position he held for 22 years. His pay was $90 a month. One of his first assignments was to lead Colonel Macleod to a suitable site for a fort from which the whisky trade could be monitored. Early in October the scout led the party westward to a large island on the Old Man River that offered natural protection, ample wood supply, and was on a well-travelled route. This fort later became known as Fort Macleod.

Potts abhorred whisky trading with the Indians, even though he himself liked to indulge. Whisky was ultimately responsible for the tragic murder of his mother and her son No Chief by another Blackfoot brave, in a drunken dispute. Jerry Potts was beloved by the Blackfoot and his many battles with them only added to his fame as a warrior and strategist.

A Man of Few Words

Jerry Potts was renowned as a man of few words. On one occasion, after burying the riddled body of an Assiniboine, he was asked the probable reason for the killing. "Drunk", he muttered. Continuing their journey to Fort Whoop-Up over the monotonous terrain, one officer asked Potts, "What do you think we'll find on the other side of this hill?" "Nudder hill", replied the laconic guide.

Little did he know that his habit of shortening words or phrases would come to play a significant role in the names of Alberta. For example, Blackfoot Chief 'Crow-big-foot' simply became Crowfoot. Potts' interpretation of the Blackfoot *Spitze* (Tall or High Timber) was High River, the name of the present town. And the southern Alberta river referred to by the Blackfoot as 'The River The Old Man Played On' was shortened by Potts to Old Man River (now the Oldman River).

The legendary Jerry Potts, about 1874. An inscription below this photo reads "Jerry Potts at Fort Macleod. Famous N.W.M.P. half-breed scout among the Blackfoot."

Mt. Evan Thomas

Mt. Packenham

Mt. Hood

Mount Evan-Thomas

Trimming the Moustache

Potts was known to partake of a few jolts of whisky with his friend George Star. Both were expert marksmen. When well-fortified with liquor, one of their favourite tricks on a $5 bet was to see who could trim the other's moustache with bullets from their revolvers at 25 paces. Time and time again both men survived this drunken prank, which led the Blackfoot to believe that Potts had supernatural powers. Once, when Star claimed a draw, Potts would have none of it. "I think not," he said. "You are going to be disqualified, my friend." Drawing his finger under his nose he showed Star some blood. "You see, you drew blood, and that ain't in the deal." Laughing, the two staggered back into the saloon for another drink!

The Death of Jerry Potts

It is amazing that Jerry Potts was never injured during all the battles in which he took part. The closest he came to being seriously wounded was during a duck hunt with Constable Tom Clarke. While hiding in thick reeds, Clarke mistakenly hit Potts in the neck with a shotgun blast. The blast knocked Potts down and left one pellet lodged in his neck behind his ear. Being superstitious and valuing good-luck charms, he refused to have the pellet removed. Years later, while drinking with some buddies, one of his group popped the pellet out with a penknife. Potts was devastated at having lost his good-luck charm. Until the day he died, he blamed his failing health on the loss of the charm.

Jerry Potts died on July 14, 1896, from tuberculosis. The Mounted Police mourned his passing with a large funeral held in Fort Macleod with full military honours. His body was laid to rest in the tiny cemetery east of town, where a small headstone marked his plot. Three volleys were fired over his grave, and a general salute was blown after each volley. If ever there was a true hero of the Canadian West, it was Jerry Potts!

Mount Evan-Thomas 3097 m

Glimpses of Mt. Evan-Thomas can be had from the Kananaskis Trail at either Grizzly Creek or Ripple Rock Creek. The mountain is connected to Grizzly Peak by a huge, broad saddle and to Mt. Potts by a jagged, exposed ridge.

Admiral Hugh Evan-Thomas

The Stoney Indians knew the valley and creek of the same name as *Ithorhan Odabi Waptan* ('Porcupine Creek'), due to the abundance of porcupines found in the valley. They also had many names for the creek, including *Cha se tida Wapta* ('Burnt Timber River') and *Kiska Tha Waptan* ('Mountain Goat Creek').

However, the Boundary Commission chose to name this highest peak of the Opal Range after Rear Admiral Hugh Evan-Thomas, who took part in the Battle of Jutland in 1916. It is widely accepted that his Fifth Battlecruiser Squadron fought gallantly and probably saved Vice-Admiral Beatty's battlecruiser fleet from disaster at Jutland. Beatty later blamed Evan-Thomas for errors in battle strategy, especially for his failure to open fire on the enemy because he had not received orders to do so. Later, a vindicated Evan-Thomas received decorations from five countries for his maritime war efforts.

A party consisting of M. Dixon, N. Gish, S.G. Pearson, and P. Rainier first ascended Mt. Evan-Thomas in July 1954, even though they thought they were climbing Mt. Packenham. This error was not corrected until 1972. Stan Pearson writes in the Canadian Alpine Journal that the party followed two groups of goats, each consisting of about six animals, up the slopes of Evan-Thomas. Upon reaching the summit the party realized that it was not the first to make the ascent. Tracks in the snow plainly showed that "The goats had actually made the first ascent and were already on their way down the east side."

Grizzly Peak 2500 m

The small peak connected to Mt. Evan-Thomas by a wide saddle overlooking the Kananaskis Trail is unofficially called Grizzly Peak. An old legend is associated with this name. Apparently a young maiden and her husband were hunting in the area, and when the husband did not return to camp, a search party was sent out to find him. They heard rifle fire and assumed it was the husband firing at a bear, but when they discovered his body, they found his jaw was snapped open and his body was mangled, with pieces scattered everywhere. A grizzly covering the parts with soil and grass had cached other parts. Hence the name *Wataga Waptan* or 'Grizzly Creek', after which the mountain was named.

Grizzly Peak from the Kananaskis Lakes Trail

Mount Packenham 3000 m

Mount Packenham, in the Opal Range, is yet another mountain named in honour of a naval commander at the Battle of Jutland. Naval records of the battle leave no clue as to why the Boundary Commission might have named this peak after Rear Admiral W.C. Pakenham (his name was misspelled by the

Mounts Packenham and Hood

Boundary Commission). Pakenham was commander of the Second Battlecruiser Squadron, and his flagship was the HMS *New Zealand* under the command of Captain John F.E. Green.

The New Zealand witnessed some of the worst destruction during the entire naval battle, but experienced very little of the action herself. An officer on the flagship described the

Mt. Brock

Mount Brock from the summit of King Creek Ridge

destruction of the HMS *Queen Mary* from very close range. As the smoke cleared, it revealed "the stern from the funnel aft afloat and the propellers still revolving, but the forward part had already gone under. Men were crawling out of the top of the after turret and up the after hatchway. When we were abreast, this after portion rolled over and blew up. Great masses of iron were thrown into the air and things were falling into the sea round us. Before we had quite passed, the *Queen Mary* completely disappeared."

Glen W. Boles, J.Pomeroy, M. Simpson, and D. Forest completed the first ascent of the mountain in 1972.

Mount Hood 2903 m

Captain Horace Hood

Mount Hood was named in honour of Rear Admiral Horace L.A. Hood, who lost his life at the Battle of Jutland when his flagship HMS *Invincible* was sunk in a vicious battle with the German battlecruiser *Derflinger*. During this battle Hood was proud of the accuracy of his gunnery crew, urging them on with praise: "Your firing is very good. Keep at it as quickly as you can: every shot is telling."

A dreadful spectacle then befell the *Invincible*. A salvo from the *Derfflinger* suddenly engulfed Hood's flagship. One of the shells pierced a turret amidships, bursting inside and then causing the magazine to ignite. The horrendous explosion ripped the *Invincible* in half. An eyewitness wrote, "She blew up exactly in half. The two ends then subsided, resting on the bottom so that they almost stood up vertically with the stem and stern standing an appreciable distance out of the water." A photo of the macabre sight can be found in the section on Mt. Invincible on pages 92-93.

It must have been a dreadful sight. Mortally wounded men screaming for help. Men desperate to save their lives diving into the ice-cold waters of the North Sea, clinging to any bit of wreckage they could find. Men drowning in the frigid waters or succumbing to hypothermia. There were only six survivors from a crew of over one thousand, but the gallant Admiral Hood was not one of them.

Mount Brock 2902 m

Rear Admiral Osmond de Beauvier Brock commanded the First Battlecruiser Squadron at the Battle of Jutland. His flagship was the battle cruiser HMS *Princess Royal*, under the command of Captain W.C. Cowan. It is not clear why the Boundary Commission chose to honour Rear Admiral Brock by naming this mountain after him. His contributions to the Battle of Jutland were minimal, barely warranting mention in the historical account of the battle.

The *Princess Royal* was armed with eight 13.5-inch guns, sixteen 4-inch guns, and two 21-inch submerged torpedo tubes. A 9-inch protective armour belt surrounded the vessel. Her top speed was 27 knots. HMS *Princess Royal* became Admiral Beatty's flagship after he transferred from the badly damaged HMS *Lion* during the Battle of Jutland.

First ascent of the mountain occurred in 1954 when P.J.B. Duffy and K. Ingold stepped onto its virgin summit. They had successfully climbed the peak via its southwest face a mere three and a half hours after leaving the Kananaskis Trail.

Mt. Blane

Mt. Blade

Mount Blane 2993 m

Considerable confusion exists over the origin of the name of Mt. Blane. Official Government of Canada documents record that it was named for Sir Cecil C.R. Blane, commander of the battle cruiser HMS *Queen Mary*, which took part in the Battle of Jutland. However, official British naval records indicate that the *Queen Mary* was commanded by Captain Cecil I. Prowse.

Although Sir Cecil Blane is recorded as dying at the Battle of Jutland, it is not known how or where this occurred. Captain Prowse died with 1,266 other seamen when the *Queen Mary* was sunk in the North Sea. Perhaps the mountain should have been named in honour of Prowse!

Sadly, the first ascent of the mountain in September 1955 by P.J.B. Duffy, D. Kennedy, G. Johnson, and F. Koch was marred by a tragedy. After surmounting two chimneys and 60 metres of exposed climbing on a knife-edge, the triumphant party stood on the unstable summit. They left it a little after 3 P.M. After they descended by the same route to a narrow ledge they had nicknamed 'The Goat Walk', there was no sign of Frank Koch, who had been bringing up the rear. A search proved to be fruitless, so the rest of the party continued their descent, hopeful that Koch would be found alive. Later the next morning, after an extensive search, his body was found. Apparently he had been struck in the head and killed instantly by rockfall, even though there were no climbers above him who could have dislodged rocks.

The Blade 2910 m

The Blade is the spectacular gendarme on the south ridge of Mt. Blane that had remained unclimbed until September 1974, when Pat Morrow and Chris Perry finally made the ascent.

About 150 feet from the summit they were forced out onto the west face and 500 feet of exposure. "Chris led it—whew!" said Morrow in his account of the climb. The last three rope lengths were memorable for the two climbers as the width of the south summit ridge narrowed dramatically to but a few feet, and in some places mere inches. Morrow went on, "Everything we touched settled into a new place or fell off either side. When we finally scooped together a summit cairn at 1 P.M., our nerves were in

Mount Blane and The Blade from King Creek Ridge

Mount Burney from King Creek Ridge

another spectacular view of the Opal Range.

Burney was described as a competent officer and a good friend of Admiral Sir John Jellicoe, Commander-in-Chief of the Grand Fleet. He had even taken over as temporary Commander of the Fleet in 1915 while Jellicoe was hospitalized with a debilitating case of piles. Jellicoe often defended Burney as a "fine seaman", while at the same time recognizing that he was slow of thought, very conservative, and not very innovative.

First ascent of the peak was a solo effort by R. Lofthouse in 1956.

worse shambles than the route we had just done. And we had yet to retrace our steps (on hands and knees) to get off of it." Morrow suggests that the next party intent on attempting this gendarme wait at least 20,000 years in order for the erosive forces of nature to clean the debris off the summit ridge.

Mount Burney 2934 m

Mount Burney, named after Vice Admiral Sir Cecil Burney, is also difficult to view from the Kananaskis Trail, as it is partially hidden by Mt. Wintour.

Mount Jerram 2996 m

Like Mt. Burney, Mt. Jerram is very difficult to view from Kananaskis Trail as it, too, is partially hidden behind Mt. Wintour. This peak was named in honour of Vice Admiral Sir Thomas Jerram, commander of the Second Battlecruiser Squadron at the Battle of Jutland. His flagship HMS *King George V* and the eight battleships under his command saw little if any action during the battle, and one has to wonder why a major peak was named in Jerram's honour.

In fact, Vice Admiral Jerram committed a colossal blunder at Jutland when he mistook German battleships for those of the Grand Fleet. "Negative", he signalled to Captain Ralph Crooke in the HMS *Caroline*. "Those ships are our battle cruisers." This was yet another missed opportunity by the Grand Fleet at Jutland to inflict serious damage to the German High Seas Fleet.

In June 1957, D.K. Morrison and J.F. Tarrant made the first ascent of Mt. Jerram. They scrambled up a wide avalanche gully for 300 metres to the west ridge, and thence up the ridge to where it merged into the west face. The west face required care as it was covered with about three inches

Mounts Jerram and Schlee

However, if you look east up King Creek Canyon near the day use area, you can catch a glimpse of it. It is the second peak to the right (south) of Mt. Blane and is easy to identify at the east end of the canyon. From the summit of King Creek Ridge there is

Mt. Wintour

of snow, and some of the rocks were covered with verglas — a thin coating of hard black ice that covers rock when meltwater freezes. It also presented considerable exposure. After climbing the smooth section and a shallow gully, and performing other awkward maneuvers, a well-placed and safe ledge was greeted by both Morrison and Tarrant as one of those "Thank God resting places." A 30-metre gap in the ridge had to be down-climbed before the summit was reached. The entire effort took over six hours from King Creek Canyon.

Mount Schlee 2850 m

Mount Schlee is a minor peak of the Opal Range, and lies between Mt. Elpoca to the south and Mt. Jerram to the north. The first ascent of the mountain was by D. Forest, G. Scruggs, G. Boles, and M. Simpson in 1976, at which time it was still unnamed. The name they proposed was in honour of their friend Gerrit Schlee (1934-1975), who died saving the life of his drowning friend in the Bow River.

Mount Wintour 2700 m

Mt. Wintour was named, like so many in the Kananaskis Lakes region, in honour of a commander at the Battle of Jutland. Captain C.J. Wintour was commander of HMS *Tipperary* of the Fourth Destroyer Flotilla at the battle.

On May 31, 1916, the Battle of Jutland carried on into the night, and it became a dreadful one. The British fleet was ill-equipped and ill-prepared for night fighting, and would pay dearly. Captain Wintour, leading in the *Tipperary*, was followed by the *Spitfire, Sparrowhawk,* and eight other destroyers, including *Broke.* As *Tipperary* challenged a German line she was suddenly lit up by a blaze of searchlights, after which she was hit by a rain of shells from the German flotilla. One hit burst the main steam pipes to the turbines, which brought the ship to a standstill. More salvos from the German cruiser *Westfalen* turned *Tipperary* into a blazing inferno. An hour later she sank beneath the waters of the North Sea. Captain Wintour and 185 men were killed. During the night the crippled *Sparrowhawk* came across a raft with 15 of Wintour's survivors, who were singing "It's a long way to Tipperary."

Mount
Wintour

Peaks of the Kananaskis Range

Olympic Summit Mt. Allan Mt. Collembola

Panorama of peaks from Nakiska Point of Interest on the Kananaskis Trail, 23.5 km from the Trans-Canada junction.

The peaks of the Kananaskis Range extend from Mt. Lorette south to the Kananaskis Lakes. Limestone and dolomite rocks of this range were formed about 350 million years ago, and are the principal peak- and cliff-forming rocks of the front ranges. These are the same strata that form the important limestone re-

Mount Sparrowhawk from the helipad at Kananaskis Village

serves used at the cement plants at Exshaw. They were formed by deposi- tions in the ancient Devonian seas hundreds of millions of years ago.

Mount Allan 2819 m

Mount Allan has had a rich and colourful history. Indeed, it is one of only a few mountains responsible for the rewriting of geological history. But first, the name. Duncan Crockford suggested it in honour of Dr. S.A.

Allan (1884-1955), the first professor of geology at the University of Alberta. Professor Allan did extensive research in the mountains of Alberta, survey- ing for coal, petroleum, and natural gas.

Prior to the mountain's official naming, the Stoney Indians knew of the mountain by two names: *Chase Tida Baha* ('Burnt timber hill') and *Wataga ipa*, because it was good griz- zly bear habitat due to the abundance of berries on its slopes.

George M. Dawson, Dominion Surveyor, investigated the geology of the Ribbon Creek area in the years 1881-1884, but it was not until 1903- 1904 that detailed work on the loca- tion and economic possibilities of the coal seams in the region was pub- lished by Bogart Dowling. He discov- ered that the coal seams belonged to the Kootenay formation, considered to be Lower Cretaceous in geological age, and varied in thickness from a fraction of an inch to over 34 feet.

The Legend of Chase Tida

Chase Tida ('Burnt timber flats') re- ferred to the prairie-like region ex- tending from the present-day Kananaskis Ranger Station to the Mt. Kidd campground. According to leg- end, a Stoney party was on an expedi- tion to trade with the Shuswap and Kootenay tribes across the Great Di- vide. The going was very rough over fallen trees, and blazing a trail was strenuous work. One of the Stoney braves named Coyote didn't like the rough going, and said he wanted to hang back in order to clear the trail some more. Two days later Coyote caught up with the party and they continued on their expedition, hunt- ing and trading.

On their way back to Stoney coun- try the group came to the place where

Coal wagon at Ribbon Creek day use area

Coyote had left them, only to discover that the area once heavily forested was now covered with barren and blackened burnt timber. Coyote had burnt the thick forest in order to clear a trail to make passage easier, and that is how *Chase Tida* got its name.

The Centennial Ridge Trail

The Rocky Mountain Ramblers built Mount Allan Centennial Ridge Trail over three summers to commemorate Canada's 1967 centennial. It was the highest trail ever built in Canada, extending 19 km from Ribbon Creek over the summit and down the north ridge to Dead Man's Flats.

Rewriting the Book

Martin Nordegg and Bogart Dowling prospected the Ribbon Creek area in 1907. Nordegg sought financial backing from Europe. When he returned to Germany in 1910 with his report on the coalfields in the Rockies and a sample of coal, Nordegg met Professor Pontonie, who had written the book on coal formation and had stated that coal does not form in rocks of Cretaceous origin. He accused Nordegg of trying to swindle him. It was only after Pontonie was invited to Canada by the Canadian Mining Institute and examined the coal in the rock formations of Ribbon Creek that he finally relented, saying, "There *is* coal in the Cretaceous. I must rewrite my book!"

It wasn't until 1947 that coal was finally mined from Mt. Allan by Brazeau Colliers, Nordegg's company, but mining in the area was short-lived. By 1952, a combination of high freight rates and low market value led to the closing of mining operations on Mt. Allan. All that remains of this legacy is the ugly mine scar on the lower slopes of the Olympic Summit, and various pieces of machinery used to mine the coal, in the Ribbon Creek parking lot.

Mt. Collembola 2800 m

Mount Collembola derives its name from the 16-eyed snow fleas that suddenly appear on the snow with the onset of warm spring weather. They are so numerous that cross-country skiers squash them by the millions, which sometimes entails rewaxing.

Mount Sparrowhawk 3121 m

Mt. Sparrowhawk was not named for the small, swift bird of prey, but rather the HMS *Sparrowhawk*, which

Mount Bogart from the bridge spanning the Kananaskis River

was a destroyer of the Fourth Flotilla, and met an untimely fate at the Battle of Jutland in 1916.

The mountain was first ascended in May 1947, from Ribbon Creek via the ESE ridge by R.C. Hind, L. Parker, and Mr. and Mrs. H.H. Rans. Today it is an easy scramble up scree slopes on the west ridge.

At the Battle of Jutland, night was descending on the battleships on the last day of May, and the British Grand Fleet was ill-prepared for night battle. The poor *Sparrowhawk* was about to become a casualty of this inadequacy. The German High Seas Fleet, on the other hand, had trained especially for night warfare.

The two summits of Mount Kidd, viewed from the south on the Kananaskis Trail at Galatea day use area, 9.4 km south of the junction to Kananaskis Village

As the Fourth Flotilla was suddenly fired upon, sister ship HMS *Broke*, directly ahead of the Sparrowhawk, was hit with a salvo just as she was turning to fire her torpedoes, jamming her helm. To the horror of her crew, the *Broke* swung quickly to port, coming straight towards the bridge of the *Sparrowhawk* at 28 knots. The impact of the two vessels was horrific. One can only imagine the screeching of metal as the two

battleships collided. The force of the collision left the *Broke* with 42 dead, 34 wounded, and 6 missing. Miraculously the *Broke* avoided being sunk by torpedoes and escaped into the darkness, reaching safety some 24 hours later.

Not so the poor *Sparrowhawk*. No sooner had she been hit by the Broke when she was rammed again at full speed a second time by HMS *Contest*. The force of this collision sliced a 30-foot piece off the helm of *Sparrowhawk* and bent the front of the *Contest* at right angles. The crippled *Sparrowhawk* actually survived these two collisions, continuing in the darkness, and even rescuing 15 crewmen from the sinking HMS *Tipperary*, commanded by Captain Wintour.

HMS *Marksman* took the *Sparrowhawk* in tow, but it soon became impossible to save her in the prevailing high seas. Commander N.A. Sullivan was then ordered by high command to sink the *Sparrowhawk* after taking on all survivors. And so the *Sparrowhawk* met her end not at the hands of the German High Seas Fleet, but due to collisions with members of her own fleet and then by torpedoes fired by her own comrades.

Mount Bogart 3144 m

Mount Bogart is the second highest peak in the Kananaskis Range. It has a distinctive pyramidal shape that makes it hard to miss. It is located almost directly south of Mt. Sparrowhawk. The mountain was named in 1904 to honor Dr. D. Bogart Dowling, a geologist from the Geological Survey of Canada who pioneered the search for coal and petroleum in the region.

The first ascent of this majestic peak occurred that eventful summer of 1930 when Katie Gardiner and Walter Feuz had their most successful trip to the Kananaskis region (see the Mt. Galatea section on page 110 for details). Camping at the south fork of Ribbon Creek near the waterfall, they scrambled up the south side of the mountain via a gully. At the top of the gully, Katie described "a wild mountain theatre with many sheep tracks. It contained a lake which was shut in by the mountain on one side and by high cliffs on the other." After ascending a crack in the southeast rock band, they reached the south ridge and then the summit in 4 3/4 hours.

The subsidiary peak 1.5 km northeast of Mt. Bogart is Ribbon Peak (2880 m). It is sometimes mistaken for Mt. Bogart because being closer to the highway it appears taller, and from some angles even hides Bogart from view. Ribbon Peak was first ascended by F.W. Crickard, R. Higgin and Hans Gmoser in 1957 via the southeast face and ridge.

Mount Kidd
2958 m

Mount Kidd stands like a guardian over the Kananaskis Valley. It is visible from as far north on the Kananaskis Trail as Barrier Lake, and from the south from as far away as Elk Pass. The mountain is actually composed of two summits, with the north summit (2958 m) slightly higher than the south (2895 m).

No record exists for the first ascent of the south peak, but R.C. Hind and J.F. Tarrant were the first to attain the summit of the main peak via the north-northwest ridge in June 1947. The 300-metre north-northeast buttress directly above the village was first ascended in June 1962 by G.W. Boles, H. Gude, and B. Greenwood.

The mountain was named in honour of Stuart Kidd. Kidd moved to Morley in 1907, where he operated the Scott and Leeson Trading Post until 1911. He became fluent in the Stoney language and was so highly respected that he was made an honourary chief and given the Stoney

name *Tah-Osa* ('Moose Killer'). Geologist D. Bogart Dowling named this prominent mountain after him.

The Stoney Called it Istimabi Iyarhe

An old Indian legend has it that a Stoney brave was hunting mountain goats on the slopes of this mountain. The goats led him ever higher up, until at last he was trapped by the steep cliffs and darkness, and had to spend the night on the mountain. At dawn he fired his rifle and was rescued by the hunting party that had spent the night below on the Kananaskis River. Since that time the mountain was called *Istimabi Iyarhe* or 'Where-one-slept mountain'.

Stuart Kidd (l), Con "Dutch" Bernhard and Wilfred Gray, circa 1920s

Mt. Lawson

Mount Lawson from Kananaskis Trail at Fortress Junction

Mount Lawson 2795 m

Mount Lawson is a rather nondescript peak 1 1/2 km southeast of Mt. Inflexible. It is named after Major W.E. Lawson, who was a member of the Geological Survey of Canada at the turn of the century and who was killed in action during World War I.

The first recorded ascent of the mountain did not occur until August 1975, when J. Martin, R. MacLauchlan, and Lynda and Lynne Howard climbed the northeast face and then the north ridge of the mountain. It was an easy scramble, and unbelievably, no summit cairn was found.

Colonel James Walker

Fortress region, including Gusty Peak and Mount Galatea

Mt. James Walker — The Fortress — Gusty Pk. — Mt.Galatea

There was Another Lawson

It is interesting to note that a Captain Robert N. Lawson commanded the light cruiser *Chester* at the Battle of Jutland. His skillful maneuvering of the *Chester* against overwhelming

odds is all that saved the cruiser and its crew from certain destruction. Mount Chester is located not far away from a mountain that has the same surname as the heroic captain of the HMS *Chester*.

The Fortress 3000 m

This spectacular view (below, left) of The Fortress with its towering 600-metre north face, shows its fortress-like appearance, and that is exactly how the peak got its name. Hans Gmoser and L. Grillmair made the first ascent of the peak in 1957. They forded the Kananaskis River and then climbed the headwall to the high col south of the summit that is visible from the highway. From there, they scrambled up easy slopes to the summit. Their descent route, the southwest ridge, is today the second most popular scramble in the Chester Lake region of Kananaskis Country.

Mount James Walker 3035 m

This peak was named to honour Colonel James Walker. First ascent of the mountain did not occur until August 1969, when J. Kuenzel, J. Martin, G. Rathborne, and F. Williamson, starting from the Fortress ski road, climbed a northeast buttress to a subsidiary peak and then scrambled easily along the southeast ridge to the top in 5 1/2 hours. At this time the mountain was still unnamed.

In September 1977 members of the Alpine Club of Canada, after climbing this yet-unnamed spectacular peak, recommended that it be named Mt. James Walker. Later that year the name was given government approval and became official.

Colonel James Walker was a man

of action and magnetism who was drawn to the west in 1874 by the newly-created North West Mounted Police. The force was looking for men who could withstand danger and hardship, nights without beds, days without meals, and storms without shelter. James Walker was such a man.

In May 1881, Walker resigned from the force to run the Cochrane Ranch Company owned by Senator Matthew Cochrane. It was at this time that Walker acquired a homestead along the banks of the Bow River about two miles southeast of old Fort Calgary. He constructed a shed for milling operations on this property in 1882, and it wasn't long before Calgary's first sawmill was in full swing. Later he became the elected 'unofficial mayor' of Calgary and was honoured as Calgary's Citizen of the Century during the city's centennial in 1975.

Mount Inflexible 3000 m

This mountain was named for the battleship HMS *Inflexible*, which took part in two major battles during World War I—the Battle of the Falklands in 1914 and the Battle of Jutland

HMS *Inflexible* had an illustrious career. She was one of three battle cruisers dispatched to the Falkland Islands in 1914 to avenge the British naval defeat at Coronel. *Inflexible* engaged the German warship *Scharnhorst* in the Battle of the Falklands in a crucial encounter, during which *Inflexible* only received three hits that caused no significant damage. Only one member of her crew was killed. The *Scharnhorst* suffered terrible damage but continued to fire salvos even while sinking. The doomed cruiser finally listed heavily to port until she "lay on her beam ends", and went down with her flag still flying. Her entire crew, including her brave

commander Von Spee and two of his sons, was lost. In 1916, *Inflexible* was a member of the Third Battlecruiser Squadron, which took part in the Battle of Jutland.

Brian Greenwood and R. Lofthouse completed the first ascent of Mt. Inflexible in 1956 via the east face, in four hours from the highway.

Gusty Peak 3000 m

Gusty Peak is the unofficial name of the pointy little peak located between Mt. Galatea and the Fortress, approximately 3 1/4 km north of Mt. Chester. It was named for the gale force winds experienced by the first ascent party in June, 1972, which was made up of G. Scruggs, P. Roxborough, G. Boles, and D. Forest. Today this is a popular scramble in the Chester Lake area.

Mount James Walker from the summit of Opal Ridge

The Tower

Mount Galatea and The Tower

You have to be quick and a bit lucky to catch a glimpse of these two gigantic peaks from the Kananaskis Trail. They form the mountain barrier at the head of Galatea Creek and are better observed from the Smith-Dorrien side of the Kananaskis Range. For that reason, the historical account of these peaks is presented in the Smith-Dorrien section (see pages 110-11).

The Legend of Katie Gardiner

Katie Gardiner

Katherine Maude Gardiner (1886-1974) was a shy, reserved lady who left a legacy in the Canadian Rockies that may never be matched. She was born to an old upper-middle-class Yorkshire family. Her father was a notable alpinist and a vice-president of the Alpine Club of London. From him Katie learned mountaineering skills at an early age. She felt duty-bound to attend to her invalid mother until her death in 1925. This hampered her climbing experiences and delayed her mountaineering exploits until she was 40 years of age, when, in 1926, she made her first excursion to New Zealand.

Fortunately for Katie, her father had invested heavily in the infant Canadian Pacific Railway, and upon his death she inherited a small fortune that allowed her to pursue her climbing career. She made her first trip to Canada in 1929, and after that she divided her climbing time between New Zealand and Canada.

Katie was a member of the Alpine Club of Canada and the American Alpine Club, and served as president of the Ladies' Alpine Club in England from 1941 to 1943. During World War II, she served in the Red Cross as a commandant of an auxiliary convalescence unit in England. In 1948 she settled down in New Zealand. She died there at her home in Hastings in January 1974.

When she arrived in Canada in 1929, Katie promptly hired Walter Feuz as her guide, and the relationship developed into a lifelong friendship. During August of that first year, Katie made five first ascents with Feuz and also climbed Mt. Assiniboine. That was only a small sign of her exploits to follow.

Katie Gardiner: What a Record!

First ascents in the Kananaskis region:

June 1930: Mt. Galatea (3185 m), Mt. Sarrail (3174 m), and Mt. Foch (3180 m).
July 1930: Warrior Mtn. (2973 m), Mt. Lyautey (3082 m), Mt. Cordonnier (3021 m), and Mt. Bogart (3144 m).

First ascents elsewhere in the Canadian Rockies:

1929: Mt. Allcantara (2840 m), Mt. Brussilof (3005 m), Mt. Prince Henry (3227 m), Mt. Prince Edward (3200 m), and Mt. Cadorna (3145 m).
1930: Mt. Unwin (3268 m), Mt. Warren (3300 m), Mt. Petain (3183 m), Mt. Mary Vaux (3201 m), Mt. Charlton (3217 m), Mt. Brazeau (3470 m), Mt. Henry MacLeod (3288 m), Mt. Coronett (3152 m), Valad Peak (3250 m), and Monkhead Peak (3211 m).
1933: Katie became the first women to climb South Goodsir (3562 m), and made the first traverse of Mt. Sir Donald (3297 m).

The 'Over the Hill Club'

Katie Gardiner had always wanted to climb Mt. Robson (3954 m). In the summer of 1937 she hired Edward Feuz Jr., and along with Christian Hasler she climbed Robson, becoming the second woman to do so. On their way back to Lake Louise, they climbed another ten mountains, an astonishing feat considering Katie was already 52 years old and both of her guides were over 50 as well. Quite a statement for what she termed the 'Over the Hill Club'. In all, Katie made 33 first ascents in Canada—a record for women, and one matched by very few male climbers.

Camping in a Crevasse

Katie was well-prepared for the hardships of the Canadian Rockies. She once spent nine days in a crevasse on a glacier in New Zealand, waiting out a blizzard, and living off dried oatmeal. It had been a clear morning in February 1933 when Katie, with guides Vic Williams and Jack Pope and climbing friend A.M. Binnie, attempted an ascent of Mt. Tasman (3498 m) in New Zealand. It would be Katie's fifth attempt of the peak; each time she had been defeated by poor weather conditions.

The group was spending the night in two tents at a bivouac site on a ridge when a terrific storm blew in. Katie was left lying on the ground after her tent blew away. The storm became so violent that people could hardly breathe. They decided to seek the safety of a small snow platform within a crevasse at 2400 metres. Katie called it 'Camp Misery'.

With enough food for three days and a little kerosene burner to melt snow, they prepared for the worst. They began rationing their food on the second day, and by the sixth day were almost out of food. Their remaining survival rations consisted of rolled oats, from which they made porridge. On the morning of the ninth day of their ordeal the storm broke and they prepared to descend, only to encounter a thick fog. Fortunately it lifted in a few hours and the group finally made contact with a rescue party.

They had been lucky to get out alive. The storm closed in once more and lasted for three weeks. Those nine days Katie Gardiner spent in the crevasse were a testament to her courage and stamina.

The Kananaskis Lakes

Upper and Lower Lakes

Kananaskis Lakes from Grizzly Peak

Today, remnants of cirque glaciers that were once part of the great glacier that filled the Kananaskis Valley can still be found along the Continental Divide.

Before the construction of the power dams, the lakes were much different. They were smaller by one third, and the water was divided into bays by peninsulas and thickly forested islands. There were seven islands: Hawke, Hogue, Cressy, Pegasus, Schooner, and two unnamed ones. All are now underwater with exception of the tip of Hawke Island. The rocky islets observed today are the tips of former peninsulas.

Prior to the dams, the Kananaskis River ran between the two lakes for about one kilometre. Two spectacular waterfalls—one 2.5 metres high at the outlet of the lake, and the other 12.3 metres high, further downstream—were destroyed in the quest for hydroelectric power. In 1858, en route to North Kananaskis Pass, Captain Palliser was inspired by this unspoiled wilderness where the "wild, beautiful Kananaskis River leapt over a ledge of rock from a height of 20 feet and rushed on its way through a dense forest of pines."

Ohe of the most spectacular views in all of Kananaskis Country is from the slopes of Mt. Indefatigable. When Palliser crossed the Lower Kananaskis Lake in August 1858 and gazed upon the falls that separated the Upper and Lower Lakes, he was in awe. His group then came "on a second magnificent lake, the Upper Kananaskis Lake, hemmed in by mountains and studded with islets, very thickly wooded."

The Kananaskis Lakes region and the entire Kananaskis Valley have been shaped and reshaped by glaciers that advanced and then retreated over great periods of geological time. The abrasive action of glaciers 20,000 years ago created the bedrock basins that would eventually become the Kananaskis Lakes. As the Kananaskis glacier began to retreat, its meltwaters filled these bedrock basins, forming the Kananaskis Lakes.

The Kananaskis Falls as they would have appeared to Palliser in 1858

The Need for Electrical Power

Calgary Power first came to the Kananaskis Valley to assess the possibility of hydroelectric power in 1912. In 1914, M.C. Hendry published a report on the storage possibilities of the lakes and was one of the first to recognize the potential beauty of the area. He stated that, "the beauty of the lake in its natural state and the extreme probability of its becoming a summer resort in the near future should not be lost sight of."

By 1927 it was evident that the Horseshoe Falls power plant on the Bow River, built in 1911, could not supply needed requirements, and the possibility of using the Kananaskis Valley for power development was explored again. By the winter of 1932, the building of the hand-hewn spillway on Upper Kananaskis Lake was underway. The spillway was designed to raise the water level and was followed ten years later by a higher dam. The 1932 dam was a 30-foot log structure.

By 1936 a channel had been cut through the riverbed almost to the top of the falls connecting the two lakes. In 1942 the dam was further raised to increase the storage capacity of the lake, sounding the death knell for the islands and the falls between the two lakes. Clearing for the reservoir on Lower Kananaskis Lake began in 1954. The reservoir was completed in 1955 and named the Pocaterra Plant. By 1955, the Interlakes Plant was completed on the upper lake.

The Legend of Schooner Island

Schooner Island was one of the seven islands that once studded the waters of the Upper Kananaskis Lake. The elders of the Stoney Nation have passed down the following legend of wild horses associated with Schooner Island.

There was a man named Gapeya who, due to his cowardice, lost many horses, which went charging off across the water to the small island with the trees. A man with a vision of the horses told the others, "I want one person who is brave, without fear, to accompany me to capture the

The Upper Kananaskis Lake as it appeared in 1911, predating the dam, with Hidden Lake in the foreground.

horses." The Kootenays had heard this declaration and were coming over the mountains from the west to capture the horses, but before they got there the same cowardly Gapeya volunteered, "I'll be the one." In due course, the horses came charging towards them. In the lead was a grey. As he galloped closer, a weird light flashed

Schooner Island before construction of the dam

from his eyes and as he whinnied and opened his jaws, there burst out flames. The sight was too much for Gapeya, who once again showed his cowardice and fell back to the shore, crying *Ki Kiha*—"Look out, Kiha." An audience watching from shore groaned in disappointment, for there were many good pintos among the herd. The horses galloped around the man with the vision, who was standing chest-deep in the water, and then they returned to the island where they kept shaking themselves all over.

The Swiss Guides:
Heroes of the Kananaskis

In the late 1890s, the Canadian Pacific Railway was attempting to exploit the 'Canadian Alps' as a tourist destination. They were persuaded to engage Swiss guides for their alpine patrons—guides who took pride in their work and were emotionally attached to the mountains. Most of their time was spent guiding in Banff and Lake Louise, but the virgin Kananaskis region soon gained their attention. They amassed a terrific record of over 170 first ascents in the Rocky Mountains, not including new routes up already-ascended peaks. Of these, 23 were first ascents of mountains in the Kananaskis region.

Edward Feuz Jr.
(1884–1981)

Edward Feuz Jr. was the oldest son of Swiss guide Edward Feuz, and was born at Interlaken in the Swiss canton of Berne. At the age of thirteen, Edward Jr. made his first ascent of the Jungfrau (4167 m), a major peak near his home. He arrived in Canada in 1903 in the employ of the CPR, became a licensed guide in 1906, and moved permanently to Canada in 1912 with his wife Martha and daughters Gertis and Heyde. In all, he made 78 first ascents of peaks in the Canadian Rockies.

His first ascents in the Kananaskis region include Mt. Joffre (3450 m), Mt. Sir Douglas (3406 m), Mt. French (3234 m), Mt. Mangin (3058 m), Mt. Robertson (3194 m), and Mt. Smith-Dorrien (3155 m). Although he disliked A.O. Wheeler, he saved him from certain death on The President after Wheeler had refused to be roped.

Walter Feuz
(1894–1985)

Walter Feuz was the younger brother of Edward Jr. After coming to Glacier House, Walter Feuz married Joanna Heimann, and their numerous offspring soon became part of the mainstream of the social and economic life of Golden, B.C. and vicinity.

Walter made twenty first ascents in the Rockies. One of his favorite clients was Katie Gardiner, with whom he ascended Prince Edward (3200 m), Prince Henry (3227 m), Mt. Foch (3180 m), Mt. Sarrail (3174 m), Mt. Petain (3183 m), Warrior Mtn. (2973 m), Mt. Lyautey (3082 m), Mt. Bogart (3144 m), and Mt. Galatea (3185 m).

Rudolph Aemmer
(1883–1973)

Rudolph Aemmer received his guiding license in 1907 and came to Canada with Ernest Feuz (another of the five Feuz brothers) in 1909. After returning to Interlaken for the first two seasons, he remained in Canada from 1912 until his retirement in 1950. He was a dashing, handsome young man who became rather famous as a double for John Barrymore in the film *Eternal Love*, which was shot at Lake Louise in 1928.

He was also very gallant. On July 16, 1921, Dr. Winthrop Stone and his wife set out to climb Mt. Eon. Leaving his wife Margaret on a ridge about 100 feet from the top, Dr. Stone reached the summit alone, but on the way back to her, he fell. Margaret watched in horror as she saw her husband silently fall over her head, strike

a ledge and roll down the mountainside out of sight. She tried unsuccessfully to reach her husband's body. Weakened by lack of food and sleep, and in shock, she became trapped on a narrow ledge at 10,500 feet. Miraculously, she survived for eight days before being rescued by a party led by Rudolph Aemmer. Margaret is said to have murmured, "Oh Rudolph, I knew you would come." Weakened by exposure and having had little food or water, she could hardly walk, so Rudolph carried her in a rope sling on his back for four hours down to treeline.

After receiving a special citation from the American Alpine Club for this heroic rescue, Rudolph philosophically stated, "Real guides cannot be heroes. When somebody gets into trouble in the mountains, we go after him, take the necessary risks, and bring him down. Nothing else counts."

Of his twenty-two first ascents of peaks in the Rockies, eight were in the Kananaskis region, and include King George (3422 m), Mt. Tipperary (2960 m), Prince Albert (3209 m), Queen Mary (3245 m), Mt. Maude (3042 m), Mt. Birdwood (3097 m), Mt. Smuts (2938 m), and Princess Mary (3084 m).

Christian Haesler Jr. (1889–1940)

Christian Haesler Jr. was a lover of nature and wildlife, and received his guiding license in 1911. The story of the Haesler family is a tragic one. The father, Haesler Sr., committed suicide after a domestic quarrel. Christian Jr.'s youngest son died in an explosion when experimenting with dynamite. Rosa, Christian Jr.'s wife, became hopelessly insane, and their eldest son died of a heart attack in the 1950s.

But perhaps the saddest tragedy of all happened in the fall of 1939 when Christian and fellow photographer Nick Morant were attacked by a female grizzly with a cub while hiking to Sherbrooke Lake. Both men managed to climb a tree, but the grizzly clawed Haesler down and he was severely mauled. Morant climbed down the tree to come to the aid of a screaming Haesler, only to have the bear attack him. In saving Haesler's life, Morant was also mauled, his left leg broken in two places. Somehow

A photo of the famous Swiss Guides all together at Lake Louise. Left to right they are: Ernest Feuz, Rudolf Aemmer, Edward Feuz Jr., Christian Hasler and Walter Feuz.

Haesler regained consciousness, and with all of the muscles of his leg exposed to the shinbone, made it back to Wapta Lake for help. Both men spent the next six months recovering in the hospital, but Haesler never fully recovered from the nightmare. Two years later he died of an apparent heart attack while fixing a roof, but everyone knew that it was really the grizzly that had killed him.

Christian Haesler had fourteen first ascents to his credit, although none of them were in the Kananaskis region.

More Gossip About the Swiss Guides

Edward Feuz Jr. once guided the famous newspaper baron William Randolph Hearst, who had come to Glacier House with his entourage of beautiful young women. That night, afraid of an approaching storm and also of bears, they persuaded Hearst to ask Edward if he would mind sleeping in their tent. The 21-year-old Edward could hardly believe his ears, and answered with a grin, "It would be my pleasure, Mr. Hearst."

The French Military Group

The French Military Group consists of a group of peaks named after French commanders of the First World War. These peaks are all on the Great Divide, on the boundary between Alberta and British Columbia. They also form the extreme southwest boundary of Kananaskis Country, anchored by the monarch of the group, Mount Joffre. Not all of these mountains are visible from the Kananaskis Trail (Hwy. 40), but a good viewpoint is at Elpoca Bridge on the Lakeview Trail north of Highwood Pass.

Field Marshall Ferdinand Foch (1851–1921)

Mount Fox 2973 m

A little confusion exists over the origin of the name of Mount Fox. It first appears on the Palliser map in 1860, although Palliser did not mention it in his journals. He may have named the mountain in honour of Lieutenant-General Sir Charles Fox (1810–1874), an engineer who was on the Council of the Royal Geographical Society and was a designer of railroads. The Boundary Commission made the first ascent of the peak in 1916.

Mount Foch 3180 m

After fighting in the Franco-Prussian War (1870–71), Ferdinand Foch became an artillery specialist on the French General Staff. As leader of the French Second Army in the First World War, his troops blocked the German advance on the city of Nancy. Foch was then promoted to commander of the Ninth Army, which he led in a successful French counter-attack at the Battle of Marne in 1914. In stopping the German advance, he prevented the fall of Paris, becoming a French hero. This success led to another promotion and he was placed in charge of the French Northern

Mt.Fox — Mt. Foch — Mt. Sarrail — Mt. Joffre — Mt. Mangin — Mt. Cordonnier — Warrior Mtn.

Army on the Western Front, a post he held through the Battle of the Somme in 1916.

During the German Spring Offensive in 1918, Foch was promoted to Allied Supreme Commander on the Western Front. Despite clashes with U.S. commander General John Pershing over troop deployment, Foch succeeded in his role as allied commander. Foch received much of the credit for masterminding the allied victory over Germany, and dictated the terms of the armistice to the Germans. After the war he was appointed president of the Allied military committee at Versailles.

Katie Gardiner and Walter Feuz ascended Mt. Foch in July 1930, the same day they ascended Mt. Sarrail. Katie wrote in the Canadian Alpine Journal, "As it was still quite early, and as Mt. Foch looked quite near through the rarefied air, we thought we would attempt a first ascent of that, too." A perpendicular rock face that went down for several hundred feet prevented them from following the south ridge connecting Mt. Sarrail with Mt. Foch. Instead, they descended to the Foch glacier and then climbed up the north side of the mountain in 4 1/2 hours from Sarrail. This was quite a feat even by today's standards.

Mount Sarrail 3174 m

Mt. Sarrail was named to honour General Maurice Sarrail (1856–1929), who was born in Carcasonne, France. He joined the French army at a very young age, and by the time of the Great War was one of France's most senior military officers. Sarrail was also a committed socialist, which made him popular within certain circles of the French public.

General Sarrail was promoted to commander of the Third Army, leading his troops at Verdun in the First World War. It was well-known that his anticlerical and radical views conflicted with a conservative and Catholic French army. Sarrail was highly critical of his commander-in-chief, Joseph Joffre, and as a result was removed from his command after his forces suffered heavy losses during a surprise enemy offensive in June 1915. His removal provoked a political storm, and Joffre was forced to give him command of the Allied troops in Salonika as an aid to Serbians. Sarrail's "conduct and reputation for political intrigue" failed to gain him confidence with political forces of the time, and he was dismissed by Prime Minister Georges Clemenceau in December 1917. Sarrail was later appointed High Commissioner to Syria.

Mt. Sarrail was first ascended in July 1930 by Katie Gardiner and Walter Feuz, from a camp at Hidden Lake.

Panorama of the French Military Group, from the summit of Mount Indefatigable

General Maurice Sarrail

Behind the Upper Lake

Mt. Foch   Mt. Sarrail   Mt. Joffre

Panorama from the summit of Grizzly Peak, with the white fang of Mt. Joffre dominating the skyline

Mount Joffre 3450 m

Like a giant fang, Mt. Joffre dominates the French Military Group. Located in the extreme southwest corner of Kananaskis Country, it is situated between Mt. Mangin and Mt. Petain, and is the highest peak between the international boundary and Mt. Assiniboine. It is not easy to view this giant tucked behind Mt. Sarrail, but if you are alert you may catch a glimpse of the peak from the Kananaskis Trail, approximately 2 km north of the Kananaskis Lakes Trail junction. However, in order to view Mt. Joffre in all its splendour, it is necessary to attain a high vantage point such as one of the ridges in the Kananaskis Lakes area or the top of Mt. Indefatigable.

This splendid mountain was named to honour Joseph Joffre (1852–1931), Marshal of France, who as Chief of the General Staff was responsible for the direction of the French war effort during the first two years of World War I.

Joffre was born in Rivesaltes, France, in 1852. He joined the army at the tender age of 18 and over the next few years served in Formosa, In-

Marshal of France, Joseph Joffre

dochina, and West Africa, and also as an instructor at the French Military School. Developing a good reputation, he was appointed a member of the Supreme War Council and director of the rear in 1910.

Joffre was appointed chief of staff in 1911, and immediately began to purge the French Army of defensively-minded commanders in favour of Plan 17, developed by Ferdinand Foch. Plan 17 involved attacking Germany at Lorraine and the southern Ardennes rather than relying on a more defensive posture. Later, he was chiefly responsible for the Allied victory in the first battle of the Marne.

Joffre was blamed for the failure to break through on the Western Front and for the heavy losses at the Battle of Verdun, and was replaced by Robert Nivelle in December 1916. Interestingly enough, Mt. Nivelle lies southeast of Mt. Joffre in the French Military Group. Even though relieved of his command, Joffre was still very popular with the French public and was promoted to the rather ceremonial post of Marshal of France. He died in 1931.

Mount Marlborough 2973 m

The HMS *Marlborough* of the First Battlecruiser Squadron was the flagship of Vice Admiral Cecil Burney during the Battle of Jutland. She was torpedoed during the night action of the battle, which caused severe damage to her boilers and reduced her speed to a maximum of 17 knots. This caused the entire First Squadron to lag seriously behind the rest of the fleet. She was escorted back to base to be refitted for battle and barely escaped an unsuccessful attack by German submarines. Her fate was the scrapyard in 1930.

The name 'Marlborough' originated from John Churchill, First Duke of Marlborough (1650–1722), the famous "Iron Duke" who defeated the French in the Wars of the Spanish Succession.

Mount Mangin 3058 m

Charles Mangin was the most aggressive of the French generals on the Western Front. His belief in offensive tactics by using overwhelming force at any cost to human life gained him the nickname 'The French Butcher'. He took part in several successful counterattacks at the Battle of Verdun, even though the victories came with a tremendous human sacrifice, and became a French national hero. Verdun was the longest battle of World War I. When it ended on December 18, 1916, the French army had suffered about 550,000 casualties. Mangin's efforts prompted quick promotion from divisional commander to leader of the French Third Army.

Mangin was one of the few senior officers who fully supported the Nivelle Offensive, a massive assault on German lines. Involving one million French soldiers on a broad front, the offensive was launched in April 1917 against the wishes of Hubert Lyautey, the French war minister, and General Henri-Philippe Pétain and Sir Douglas Haig. On April 16, Mangin led the French forces in the disastrous attack at the Battle of Aisne, in which the French suffered over 40,000 casualties on the first day. Full-scale attacks continued with small gains until May 5, when Mangin's forces finally secured a 4-km ridge at great cost to human life. By the time the Second Battle of the Aisne had ended, the French Army had suffered 187,000 casualties. Mangin was relieved of his command in 1918, but he was later recalled as head of the Tenth French Army. By then, however, with the Ger-

mans in full retreat, conditions were more conducive to his aggressive tactics. Mangin also led the Tenth French Army in the successful second battle of the Marne. He died in 1923.

Mount Cordonnier 3021 m

Mount Cordonnier was named to honour World War I French General Emilien Victor Cordonnier. Why does this French general warrant such a monument? Only the members of the 1916 Boundary Commission hold the answer to that question.

Katie Gardiner and Walter Feuz made the first ascent of the peak in July 1930, via the easy south ridge. The summer of 1930 was a great one for the two climbers. They ascended Warrior Mountain in combination with Mt. Cordonnier, a feat that took a little less than 7 1/2 hours.

Warrior Mountain 2973 m

Warrior Mountain straddles the Great Divide directly west of the Upper Kananaskis Lake. When viewed from the Upper Lake, Warrior looks like a giant fist raised in defiance, and the

Mounts Marlborough, Mangin, and Cordonnier from the summit of Mount Indefatigable

General Charles Mangin

Warrior Mtn.

Mt. Northover

A splendid view of two peaks that straddle the Great Divide, from the Upper Kananaskis Lake parking lot

name seems appropriate. The Stoney Indians referred to the mountain as *Waka Nambe*. *Waka* is the Great Spirit, and *Nambe* means thumb. George Patterson (1961) says that it may be freely translated as 'The Hand of God'. It is truly a shame that this beautiful Stoney name was not considered by Wheeler and the Boundary Commission in the naming of this mountain. Today *Waka Nambe* refers to a minor peak just west of what was named Warrior Mountain.

Mt. Putnik

Mount Putnik

The Boundary Commission named the peak in honour of HMS *Warrior*, commanded by Captain Vincent B. Molteno. *Warrior* was the second battleship to bear that name, and the first of a class of modern battleships that featured iron construction, steam propulsion, heavy armour, and heavy guns that fired explosive shells. She was a member of the 1st Battlecruiser Squadron at Jutland led by Rear Admiral Sir Robert Arbuthnot in

his flagship HMS *Defence*.

The first battleship to bear the name *Warrior* entered the Royal Navy in 1864. She, too, was revolutionary in that she was the first armoured ship to be constructed of iron covering a teak hull. Relying on both steam and wind, she could maintain a healthy 14 knots. She has been completely restored and is on display to the public at Portsmouth Dockyard.

At the Battle of Jutland, both HMS *Warrior* and HMS *Defence* fought a courageous if futile battle against the awesome force of both Scheer's and von Hipper's battleships. Within minutes, *Defence* met with almost instantaneous destruction. An officer on the *Warrior* described a horrible scene in which the entire profile of the *Defence* "seemed to lose its definition as her sides burst away. Then the entire ship was blown into the air, deck plates, bodies, and debris being plainly visible against the smoke. When the smoke had cleared there was nothing to be seen, only the open, cold North Sea where the *Defence* had once been." Losses were high—903 officers and men, including Captain Stanley V. Ellis and Rear Admiral Arbuthnot, lost their lives.

Arbuthnot's accompanying cruiser, *Warrior*, then took the brunt of the German attention, and reeled under the blows of fifteen heavy shells. Set on fire and disabled due to a wrecked engine room, the *Warrior* survived due to the misfortune of the *Warspite*, which drew the enemy fire. The *Engadine* attempted to tow her back to port, but heavy seas eventually sank the cruiser after her survivors had been rescued. Seventy-one men from the *Warrior* lost their lives in the battle.

Mount Lyautey 3082 m

Mount Lyautey is named after General Herbert Lyautey (1854–1934). Lyautey joined the French Army early

Mt. Lyautey

in life and held administrative posts in Algeria, Tonking, and Madagascar. During the early stages of World War I he was commissary-general in Morocco before becoming the French war minister in 1916 in the government of Aristide Briand.

Katie Gardiner and Walter Feuz made the first ascent of the mountain in July 1930. From a camp at Aster Lake, they traversed the south side of the mountain to gain the south ridge, which they ascended until rotten rock and scree forced a traverse on the west face. They climbed that face to the summit in five hours.

General Lyautey was one of the few high-ranking officers appalled by the human slaughter of the ill-conceived Nivelle Offensive during World War I. During one of his visits to the Western Front he became convinced that the Nivelle Offensive was a huge mistake. Unable to convince political leaders to stop the offensive, he resigned from office in March 1917. He then returned to his post in Morocco, where he successfully developed Casablanca as a seaport.

Mount Northover
3003 m

Mount Northover is another spectacular peak on the Great Divide. It is one of only three peaks in the Kananaskis area that honours a Canadian army officer of the First World War. Lieutenant A.W. Northover was with the 28th Battalion of the Canadian Expeditionary Force in 1917. He was awarded the Victoria Cross for exceptional courage and bravery in battle.

The mountain was not climbed until 1957 — testament to its daunting nature. In July of that year, P.J.B. Duffy, S.A. Heilberg, R.C. Hind, P. Rainier, and Miss. I. Spreat were successful in their summit attempt via the south ridge, which included a knife-edge that angled off at over 40 degrees. Alan Kane says that "apart from falling off, there is no quick way down from this south ridge."

Mount Putnik
2940 m

Mount Putnik was named by the Boundary Commission in honour of the "Distinguished Serbian" Radomir Putnik (1847–1917). Born in Kraguyevats, Serbia, Putnik became the first Serbian duke and army commander. He began his military career against the Turks in 1876 and served in the war against the Bulgarians in 1889. He was then appointed deputy-chief of the Serbian General Staff and

Mount Lyautey from the North Interlakes day use area

Minister of the Serbian Army, planning the strategy for the coming Balkan Wars.

A series of political intrigues and a falling-out with the Serbian monarchy led to his retirement. However, a military revolt in the same year resulted in his promotion to Chief of the General Staff and then in 1906 he assumed the additional role of Minister of War. In 1912 he became the first Serbian ever to be appointed Field Marshall of the Serbian forces.

After serving in the First and Second Balkan Wars of 1912–1913, Putnik's health broke down and he was taken into the custody of the Austrian police. In a gesture of misplaced chivalry, Emperor Franz

Field Marshall Putnik

Joseph had him released, a move the emperor would later regret.

Once again assuming command of Serbia's army, Putnik masterminded the defeat of the Austrian invasions in 1914 and completely drove the Austrians out of Serbia by the end of that year. In 1915 a combined force of Germans, Austrians, and Bulgarians invaded Serbia and forced the retreat of the Serbian army across the mountains into Albania, where a government-in-exile was formed. Poor health continued to plague Putnik, and he died in Nice in May 1917 in his 70th year, without ever returning to his liberated homeland.

The Battle of Jutland
May 31 – June 1, 1916

So many of the peaks in the Kananaskis region were named by A.O. Wheeler and the Boundary Commission after admirals and battleships that took part in the Battle of Jutland. A brief review of this momentous naval battle will serve to explain how these names have become part of the lore of the Kananaskis. Whether or not one agrees with this naming scheme, the names are official and we must live with them.

When the First World War began in 1914, Great Britain was still the world's dominant naval power. Part of the German strategy was to lure the Royal Navy into a battle in German territorial waters, where it was hoped that a combination of submarine attacks and underwater mines would reduce the British fleet to a level of parity with the German High Seas Fleet.

The mandate of Great Britain's Grand Fleet was to form a blockade, preventing the German High Seas Fleet access to the North Sea and the North Atlantic shipping lanes. Annoyed by this blockade and his own fleet's inactivity, German Admiral

Reinhard Scheer developed a plan in which small pieces of the Grand Fleet would be lured out of port, where they could be destroyed by U-boats and battle cruisers of the German High Seas Fleet.

These two great navies were to meet at Jutland Banks off the west coast of Denmark, in a naval battle that forever became known as the Battle of Jutland. It was arguably one of the greatest naval battles in history, bringing together 150 battleships of the Great Britain's Grand Fleet against 99 battleships of the German High Seas Fleet. The battle began at 2:38 P.M. on May 31, 1916, and lasted through the night into the next day.

During this naval battle, fourteen ships of the Grand Fleet and eleven ships of the High Seas Fleet were sunk. Britain suffered 6,097 casualties and 510 wounded, while Germany suffered 2,551 casualties and 507 wounded.

The Grand Fleet

The Grand Fleet, made up of 150 warships, was the brainchild of Admiral Sir Jackie Fisher (see page 56). It consisted of four battle squadrons: a battlecruiser squadron, two cruiser squadrons, and a light cruiser squadron. The battlecruiser squadron under Admiral John Jellicoe was based at Scapa Flow, the Orkney Islands harbour off the northern coast of Scotland. The cruiser squadrons commanded by Vice Admiral Sir David Beatty were moored at Portsmouth off the east coast of Britain.

The Grand Fleet operated under the policy of containing the German High Seas Fleet against access to the North Sea and North Atlantic by means of blockade. This blockade had resulted in a number of minor skirmishes, culminated in the Battle of Jutland, and was maintained until the end of World War I.

The German High Seas Fleet

The German High Seas Fleet was moored in Jade Bay and at the mouths of the Elbe and Weser Rivers on the northern coast of Germany. The fleet was organized into three battle squadrons, with a separate battle cruiser squadron. At the beginning of the war, in 1914, it consisted of over 150 battleships. The British blockade severely limited its effectiveness, and after two early cruiser actions in which the Germans came off for worse, their commander Admiral von Ingenhol was relieved of his duties for risk-taking and was replaced by Reinhard Scheer in January 1916.

The new German commander-in-chief immediately instigated a change in policy as well as an upwelling of morale in the officers and crewmen of the navy. Greatly outnumbered in both warships and gunnery by Great Britain's Grand Fleet, Scheer's plan for the High Seas Fleet was to entice and then engage isolated British squadrons into conflict without risking an all-out conflict of forces. Little did he know that on the date of this major battle, the British had already put to sea almost their entire naval force.

First Blood

On the afternoon of May 31, 1916, both fleets were out scouting in the North Sea and nearly missed each other. Admiral Beatty had not sighted any enemy ships and had ordered his squadron to turn northward, away from the hunt. HMS *Galatea* had missed this signal to turn and continued on her original eastward course.

About this time the German light cruiser *Elbing* had stopped a Danish tramp steamer, *N.J. Fjord*, to investigate. At 3:20 P.M. the *Galatea* spotted the *Elbing* and hoisted the general flag, 'Enemy in sight'. Action stations were manned and the *Galatea* opened fire. The *Elbing* returned the fire, drawing first blood when her salvos hit the *Galatea* just below the bridge, but did little damage. It might be said that the innocent presence of a tramp steamer was the immediate cause of the Battle of Jutland.

The Fleets Collide

Admiral Beatty inadvertently led his battle cruisers into a trap set by Admiral Franz von Hipper, who made them pay dearly. Within three minutes of opening fire, HMS *Lion* and HMS *Tiger* were hit by accurate German fire, and in less than seventeen minutes, the Von der Tann hit HMS *Indefatigable* eleven times, sinking her.

Shortly after this, the battle cruiser HMS *Queen Mary* was sunk by the sustained action of the *Derfflinger*. An eyewitness saw "a dull red glow amidships and then the ship seemed to open out like a puff ball when one squeezes it." The stern of the *Queen Mary* projected out of the water some seventy feet, with her propellers still revolving, and then there was a stupendous explosion as she disappeared. She went down with 1,266 men, including her Captain, Cecil Prowse. As Admiral Beatty watched these two great battle cruisers being catastrophically destroyed, he turned to his flag captain. "Chatfield," he said, in one of the immortal sayings of British naval history, "there seems to be something wrong with our bloody ships today."

By the time battle cruiser squadron led by Jellicoe had come to Beatty's defence, HMS *Warrior* was heavily damaged, HMS *Defense* was sunk, and HMS *Invincible* was blown in half. The battleship portion of the battle began with a tremendous advantage to Jellicoe, and he soon caused heavy damage to the German warships. As the duel continued, Scheer made two brilliant moves under the cover of a smokescreen to escape the onslaught. In the meantime, von Hipper's cruisers were still inflicting heavy damage on Beatty.

Night Action

As darkness fell, both fleets were converging on each other blindly, with terrible consequences. The German High Seas Fleet was much better prepared for night action, with better coordination and searchlights. Before morning dawned, HMS *Sparrowhawk* was sunk after being rammed not once but twice by two of her own fleet. HMS *Fortune*, HMS *Black Prince*, and HMS *Ardent* were also sunk. The High Seas Fleet also suffered heavy losses but was able to escape, and the Battle of Jutland ended with both sides limping home to their respective ports, claiming victory.

Who Won?

The British blockade of the North Sea remained intact to the end of war. The High Seas Fleet would never become a force again. Germany lost over 2,000 men and eleven warships. British propaganda gave the victory to the Royal Navy.

On the other side, the High Seas Fleet had inflicted over 6,000 British casualties and sunk fourteen warships, with much more tonnage loss than it had suffered itself. German propagandists gave the victory to the High Seas Fleet.

Sometimes who won or lost a battle cannot be measured by casualties or battleships sunk. One thing is for certain—after Jutland, the High Seas Fleet was never again a force to be reckoned with, and the British blockade of the North Atlantic remained for the duration of the war. Who won the Battle of Jutland? You be the judge!

Commanders of the British Grand Fleet

Admiral of the Grand Fleet Sir John Jellicoe

Although the Battle of Jutland was a strategic victory for Britain, Admiral Jellicoe could claim no more than a tactical draw — something that was to haunt him (unfairly, one might add) with the British press and public for his entire life. His tactic of turning away, fearing German torpedo and U-boat attack, rather than risking destruction or reduction of superiority of the Grand Fleet certainly did not lose him the Battle of Jutland, but it did not win him many friends, either. One thing, however, is certain. He may not have won the battle outright in the eyes of the public, but neither did he lose it. A major naval loss at Jutland would have changed the fortunes of World War I in favour of Germany.

To most of the British public, Jutland was a major disappointment due to the fact that the High Seas Fleet had escaped annihilation. Jellicoe became the scapegoat, being criticized for his over-cautious attitude and his unwillingness to engage the enemy to the fullest. However, he could have lost the war in a single afternoon, and thus his primary objective of preventing the destruction of the Grand Fleet was justified.

Vice Admiral David Beatty

David Beatty became Vice Admiral of the Grand Fleet's battle cruiser squadron in 1913. This squadron was a force swift enough to reconnoiter and find the enemy, and strong enough to hold the enemy until the main battle cruiser force could arrive. Beatty's flagship was HMS *Lion*.

The Battle of Jutland brought out the best and worst in Beatty. His squadron suffered major losses to von Hipper because Beatty refused to wait for support, but by engaging the enemy forces he did prevent the German fleet from advancing.

Beatty was generally acclaimed the hero of Jutland over the more cautious-minded Jellicoe. Nevertheless, when Beatty succeeded Jellicoe as commander of the Grand Fleet, he followed the latter's cautious policy.

Commanders of the German High Seas Fleet

Admiral Reinhard Scheer

Reinhard Scheer (1863–1928) joined the German navy in 1872 and toiled for twenty-five years before becoming second-in-command of a ship. In 1907 he was appointed commander of a destroyer flotilla, where he specialized in torpedo warfare. Two years later, he was promoted to chief of staff of the battleship fleet. In 1916 Scheer became Commander-in-Chief of the German High Seas Fleet, when von Pohl was struck down with a serious illness. During the Battle of Jutland, Scheer demonstrated superior skill in extricating himself from superior British forces, thus saving the bulk of his fleet.

In 1918 Scheer was appointed head of the new German supreme command, in charge of authorizing a massive new submarine construction program. After his retirement, a deranged ex-soldier committed an act of violence, killing Scheer's wife and maid at their home. Scheer arrived in time to save his seriously wounded daughter, but was never the same after this incident. Broken, the old soldier committed suicide.

Admiral Reinhard Scheer

Admiral Franz von Hipper

Admiral von Hipper (1863-1932) revealed his considerable skill at the Battle of Jutland when he outmanoeuvred Beatty and destroyed two battle cruisers without sustaining any losses himself. When the tide began to turn against the Germans, von Hipper

Admiral Franz von Hipper

threw himself against the entire Grand Fleet in an effort to save the High Seas Fleet. Von Hipper succeeded Scheer as the last commander of the High Seas Fleet, and retired from the navy after having to witness the painful surrender and subsequent destruction of the German fleet at Scapa Flow in Scotland.

The Battleship Peaks

Mt. Indefatigable   Mt. Invincible   Mt. Warspite

The battleship peaks of the Spray Range

The peaks bordering the Smith-Dorrien drainage system represent a history of naval warfare during the Great War. Due to its fixation with the battles of that war, the Boundary Commission named many of these mountains after battleships of the Royal Navy. These ships were a powerful symbol of nationhood, and here they stand today, a powerful symbol of the gigantic forces of nature that formed these mountains. The battleship peaks of the Spray Range — Indefatigable, Inflexible, Warspite, Black Prince, and Shark — border the valley south of Smith-Dorrien Creek, while peaks of the Kananaskis Range — Kent, Chester,

Galatea, and Engadine — form the ramparts on the northern approaches to the valley. They flank the valley in a way reminiscent of the Grand Fleet forming battle lines in a major naval encounter. Each has a story to tell.

Mount Indefatigable 2670 m

The Boundary Commission of 1916 headed by A.O. Wheeler named thirteen of the peaks in Kananaskis Country after battleships that took part in the Battle of Jutland during World War I. Five of these peaks are part of the Spray Range, forming the southern barrier of the Smith-Dorrien Valley, and one of them, the double-peaked Mt. Indefatigable, looms over the Upper Kananaskis Lake.

The Stoney Indians knew the mountain as *Ubithka mabi* ('Mountain of the nesting eagles'). *Mabi* in the Stoney language refers to eagles with white patches under their wings.

The Boundary Commission

named the peak in honor of HMS *Indefatigable*, a battle cruiser sunk during the Battle of Jutland. She was part of the Second Battlecruiser Squadron at Jutland, commanded by Captain C.F. Sowerby, and has the ominous distinction of being the first battleship to be sunk at Jutland. This class of battleship was the cheapest built for the Royal Navy, and suffered from the same weakness as the *Invincible*—lack of protecting armour.

Perhaps the most famous ship named *Indefatigable* was the forty-four-gun, 18th-century British frigate commanded by Sir Edward Pellew, which destroyed the French battleship *Droits de L'Homme* during the Napoleonic War in 1797. This was the same frigate on which C.S. Forrester's fictional sailor Horatio Hornblower learned his trade.

The north peak of Mt. Indefatigable (2670 m) is slightly higher than south peak (2646 m), and a curving ridge connects the north peak to an outlier (2484 m) overlooking the Lower Kananaskis Lake. All are popular scrambles reached by the steep Indefatigable hiking trail.

No recorded first ascent of the mountain exists, but there is a record of Walter Wilcox setting up a camera tripod on the south summit in 1901. Wilcox described "several hundred yards of knife-edge" leading to the summit. Although it isn't quite that long or narrow, it is an apt description. Views from the summit just might be the most spectacular in all of Kananaskis Country.

Fighting Her Last Fight

Two direct hits from the *Von der Tann* quickly sealed the fate of the *Indefatigable*. Explosion of these shells sent tongues of flames into her magazines, resulting in a violent explosion about thirty seconds later. This sent debris higher than her mastheads. The main explosion started with sheets of flame, followed almost immediately

by a dense dark smoke that obscured the ship from view. Listing badly to port, she sank with startling suddenness just seventeen minutes after entering the battle. Only her captain, C.F. Sowerby, and two of her crew of 1,020 survived the shattering explosion.

HMS Indefatigable

Gypsum Mining

The announcement of deposits of gypsum on the slopes of Mt. Indefatigable, published in a 1964 report by the Geological Survey of Canada, caused a stir in the mining community. The Canadian Pacific Oil and Gas Company applied for a permit and received a 21-year lease to mine the site. The lease was eventually assigned to Alberta Gypsum, which undertook the daunting task of building a road to the mine site near the summit. The first road ended in failure, but the second one, constructed at considerable cost along the northern slopes of the mountain, can be seen today as a thin line traversing the slope.

Despite all this effort, only one carload of gypsum was ever removed from the mine. The deposit had proved to be of poor commercial quality. The Alberta government cancelled the lease, and with the formation of Kananaskis Country, forbade all mining within its boundaries. The old access road is now overgrown with encroaching vegetation but offers the hiker a pleasant and easy stroll into the subalpine.

Mt. Indefatigable

Mount Indefatigable from the summit of King Creek Ridge

Mt.Invincible

Mount Invincible from Elpoca Bridge on the Valley View Trail (top)

HMS *Invincible* as she appeared before she fought her last battle (middle)

The ghastly sight of the two ends of the *Invincible* (bottom)

Mount Invincible
2730 m

Mount Invincible was named in honour of her namesake battle cruiser, a member of the Grand Fleet. The *Invincible* took part in two major battles: she was the flagship of Vice Admiral Doveton Sturdee at the Battle of the Falklands in 1914, and the flagship of Rear Admiral H.L.A. Hood of the Third Battlecruiser Squadron at Jutland in 1916. She suffered from the same main weakness as her sister ships — in the interest of speed, their armour was too thin to provide adequate protection. The glory of *Invincible's* victory at the Falklands would be overshadowed by her fate at Jutland in 1916.

Glory in the Falklands

The *Invincible* and *Inflexible* were sent to the Falkland Islands to reinforce the British flotilla moored there, and to avenge the humiliating loss at

Coronel, Chile. On the day after Vice Admiral Sturdee arrived in the Falklands, the die was set.

First, the two British ships concentrated their fire on the German flagship *Scharnhorst*. By 3:30 in the afternoon of August 8, 1914, the *Scharnhorst* was a blazing wreck, and her captain signaled the *Gneisenau* to try to get away if her engines were still intact. Lieutenant Commander Bingham on the *Invincible* described the *Scharnhorst's* end. "She rolled quietly over on one side, lay on her beam ends, and then took a headlong dive, bow first" into the icy waters of the South Atlantic. During this encounter the *Invincible* had been hit twenty-two times, but surprisingly, did not suffer a single casualty. Seven hundred and fifty seamen went down with the *Scharnhorst*.

The two British battle cruisers next concentrated their fire on the German battle cruiser *Gneisenau*. Battered and blazing under a hail of fire, the *Gneisenau* continued to fight until the very end. As she capsized, about 300 men began to sing "Deutschland über Alles" as they jumped into the water, clinging to anything they could in order to save their lives. Most of the men perished from hypothermia in the frigid waters. Vice Admiral Sturdee sympathized with the surviving officer of the *Gneisenau*, stating, "We sympathize with you in the loss of your Admiral and so many officers and men. Unfortunately the two countries are at war; the officers of both navies, who can count friends in the other, have to carry out their countries' duties which your Admiral, Captains and officers worthily maintained to the end."

After the battle, Sturdee wrote, "It was an interesting fight, a good stand-up fight, and I always like to say I have great regard for my opponent, Admiral Von Spee. At all events he gave our squadron a chance by calling on me the day after I arrived."

Sinking the Invincible

A much different fate awaited the *Invincible* at Jutland. She was engaged in heavy fire with the leading ships of the enemy when Admiral Hood gave what would be his last command to his gunnery officer: "Your firing is very good, keep at it as quickly as you can; every shot is telling!" The end then came with dreadful swiftness. *Invincible* was hit by salvos from both the *Derfflinger* and the *Lutzow* with devastating effect. As a salvo engulfed Hood's flagship, with a shell penetrating one of the midship turrets, flames burst inside the ship, igniting the magazines. In a succession of heavy explosions, masts collapsed, all manner of debris was thrown skyward, and a gigantic column of black smoke rose skyward.

Tremendous explosions ripped *Invincible* in two and she sank almost immediately, with bow and stern projecting vertically out of the shallow North Sea for at least half an hour. When Jellicoe passed this macabre sight, he asked, "Is this wreck ours?" "Yes," came the reply. Rear Admiral Hood and 1,026 officers and crew had been lost.

Mount Maude 3042 m

Mount Maude was named in honour of Lieutenant General Sir Frederick Stanley Maude (1864–1917). Born at Gibraltar and educated at Eton, Maude was made a Major, and commanded the Coldstream Guards in the Boer War. Returning to England for medical reasons, he was appointed military secretary to the Governor General of Canada, Lord Minto, in 1901. He returned to England in 1904 and was promoted to Colonel in 1911.

During World War I, Maude was put in charge of the 14th Brigade on the Western Front, and was seriously wounded in action. After his recuperation in England he was promoted to

Major General and took command of the remains of the 13th Division on the Gallipoli peninsula. Maude and his division suffered casualties of over fifty per cent, and were transferred to Mesopotamia in March 1916.

Maude served in various commands in Europe, and finally, as Lieutenant General in charge of the Anglo-Indian forces, led a series of offensives that defeated Turkish forces in the capture of Baghdad. While still in Baghdad, Maude was stricken with cholera and died shortly thereafter in 1917 amid unfounded rumours that he had been poisoned.

First Ascent

On August 6, 1922, R. Aemmer, Miss N.B.D. Hendrie, Miss M.P. Hendrie, Miss J.B. Wilcox, C.R. Adams, E.W. Crawford, W. Gillespie and M.D. Geddes overcame high angled rock to conquer Mt. Maude. Relying almost solely on foot and finger friction, their progress was slow but steady. After reaching what they thought was the summit, they encountered a higher peak further on, separated by a thin, jagged knife-edge. *Au cheval,* they reached the top after seven hours of climbing.

Lingering on the summit, the party was then met by every climber's nightmare—a terrific thunderstorm. Geddes thought it was truly grand to witness a thunderstorm from the top of a mountain, but all Aemmer wanted to do was "get out of here!" As they crossed the knife-edge, the flashes of lightning were dangerously close, and a buzzing sound was heard coming from the soles of the

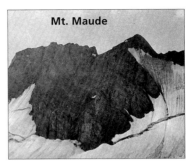

Mt. Maude

You will have to hike to the Haig Glacier in order to obtain this view of Mount Maude.

Lieutenant General Sir Maude

hobnailed boots in their rucksacks. In the true manner of a mountain man, Geddes wrote, "The air was charged with electricity and the jagged stabs of lightning were playing all around to the mighty cracking music of Heaven's dread artillery." Retreating to safety, the group waited out the storm and then descended the mountain.

Peaks of the North Kananaskis Pass

Mount Beatty

Mount Beatty 2999 m

Mount Beatty lies on the Great Divide, just north of South Kananaskis Pass. It is the highest peak on this ridge, with a pic-

Panorama of peaks in the North Kananaskis Pass region

turesque glacier descending towards North Kananaskis Pass. It was named in honour of the famous British Admiral, Sir David Beatty. The Boundary Commission of 1916 first ascended the peak, and later, in 1919, J.W.A.

Hickson, A.C. Stead, and Walter Feuz reached the summit via the north ridge in three hours.

Beatty was born in Nantwich in 1871 and entered the Royal Navy in 1884. He was as controversial as he was courageous. His valour and dashing style in the Sudan and at the Boxer Rebellion saw him created Captain at the age of 29, the youngest officer of the Royal Navy for over a century.

Taking great risks, he played a major role in the battle at the Heligoland Bight in August 1914, and achieved an early victory in which three German light cruisers were sunk. At Dogger Bank on January 24, 1915, Beatty, with five battle cruisers, surprised a powerful German force, sinking the *Blucher* and seriously damaging the *Seyditz* and *Derfflinger* before they escaped due to poor communications.

Admiral Beatty will forever be remembered in the annals of British naval history for uttering the famous remark to his flag captain: "Chatfield, there appears to be something wrong with our bloody ships today," as he watched the *Queen Mary* explode and disappear beneath the icy waters of the North Sea.

Beatty succeeded Jellicoe after the Battle of Jutland as commander of the

Grand Fleet until 1919, but he never had a second chance to defeat the German fleet. He did, however, have the pleasure of accepting the surrender of the High Seas Fleet on November 2, 1918, giving the famous signal: "The German flag will be hauled down at sunset, and will not be hoisted again without permission." At the end of the war he was created an earl and received other honours in recognition of his service with the Grand Fleet.

Beatty became First Sea Lord in 1919 and held the post until he retired in 1927. He died in 1936 at the age of 65.

The Lion almost Didn't Roar

HMS *Lion* and her sister ships, the *Princess Royal* and the *Queen Mary*, were known as the 'Splendid Cats' because of their maximum speed of 28 knots and their beautiful, slender appearance. At Jutland, the *Lion*, Beatty's flagship, no sooner entered the battle than she was hit by two salvos from the *Lutzow*, causing fires and damage to her sick bay. These were minor and the *Lion* continued a gallant battle with the German cruisers. But at 1600 hours the *Lion* was hit by a fourth salvo that pierced the roof of the midship turret, detonating inside and killing or mortally wounding the entire gunhouse crew. If not for the heroic actions of a mortally wounded Major F.J.W. Harvey, the *Lion* would have exploded much like the *Queen Mary* and the *Indefatigable*.

Harvey, mortally wounded as he had lost both of his legs, had but a few minutes to live. With his dying breath he gave the order to close the magazine doors and flood the magazine, thereby preventing the cordite from exploding. This action saved the *Lion* from utter disaster. Later, men were found still clinging to the door clasps, but they had done their heroic duty before dying. All but two of the turret gun crew perished in this disaster, and Harvey's splendid action and presence of mind earned him a posthumous Victory Cross.

Mount Jellicoe 3246 m

John Rushworth Jellicoe, son of a sea captain, was born at Southampton on December 5, 1859. He joined the British navy as a sea cadet at the age of 14, serving in Egypt in 1882. He narrowly escaped death on three occasions: from a crowd of hostile fellaheen after the bombardment of Alexandria in 1882; from the *Victoria*, when she was sunk in a collision with the *Camperdown* in 1893; and then during the Boxer Rebellion in 1900, when he was severely wounded.

Jellicoe became a captain at the age of 35, taking command of the Atlantic Fleet and then the Home Fleet. His expertise in gunnery won him rapid promotion, and he became the Third Sea Lord in 1908. At the age of 55 he was appointed Commander-in-Chief of the Grand Fleet. He worked very closely with Lord Jackie Fisher to reform and modernize the British navy in the development of new battleships, torpedo boats, and submarines.

Jellicoe was a charming man. If he had a fault, it was an inability to delegate authority to others. He thus became too concerned with minor details, rather than the broader scope of his duties. His attempts to do everything himself may have cost him dearly at the Battle of Jutland. After the war Jellicoe was relieved of his duties and was governor of New Zealand from 1920 to 1924. He received a peerage, and as Earl John Rushworth Jellicoe, Admiral of the Fleet, died in 1935.

Admiral Sir David Beatty

Sir John Rushworth Jellicoe

The Highwood Pass Region

Highwood Pass

Panorama of the alpine setting at the summit of Highwood (top)

The Highwood Pass (right)

When you reach Highwood Pass you are entering *Nyahe-ya-nibi thi*, or 'Go-up-into-the-mountain country'. Here, you will feel you are in the heart of the mountains, and sense a great silence and wonder at being surrounded by giant peaks on all sides. The air is clean and exhilarating, the water crystal-clear and ice-cold. In autumn, the alpine larches dominate the splendour. Then there is the aroma of the alpine—a unique scent that invigorates the mind and soul. There is nothing that compares to the high country!

The Highest Highway in Canada

Highwood Pass, reached by the Kananaskis Trail, takes the traveller quickly into the spectacular environs of the subalpine ecoregion. From its junction with Kananaskis Lakes Trail, Highway 40 climbs over 500 metres to the summit of Highwood Pass. This section of Highway 40 has the distinction of being the highest paved and maintained highway in Canada. The elevation is 2206 metres at the summit of the pass. This is basically the

Bighorn sheep

same route used by George Pocaterra to travel from his ranch near Eden Valley to the Kananaskis Lakes for hunting, fishing, and trapping. Each year the highway is closed from December 1 through June 15 to accommodate the elk calving season.

An alternative, short side trip to Highwood Pass is to take Valley View Trail, located 5 km south of the Kananaskis Lakes Trail junction. Be forewarned, however — this short alternative is narrow, windy, dusty, and unpaved. The rewards are two spectacular viewpoints of the Kananaskis Lakes and the mountains surrounding the lakes at Elpoca and Lakeview day use areas.

It is not clear how the name of the river or the pass originated. David Thompson in 1814 referred to Highwood River as Spitchee, while on Palliser's maps the river is referred to by the Stoney name *Ispasquenhow*. Frank Powderface, in *Stoney Place Names*, states that the Stoney referred to the Highwood River as *Cha hathka thka Wapta*, or 'Tall Trees River', after the tall aspen groves found along the river at its eastern opening.

Regardless, the source of the Highwood River is found in the pass, and is formed by the confluence of Storm and Mist Creeks.

The area surrounding the pass is spectacular, containing some of the

Grizzly bear

most scenic landscapes in all of Kananaskis Country. Glacial events have played a major role in shaping the Highwood drainage basin, but our knowledge of its glacial history is still being investigated. Highwood Pass has something for everyone: majestic

Gap Mtn.

Elpoca Mtn.

Panorama of Gap and Elpoca Mountains

peaks for scramblers, as well as strenuous hikes, easy interpretive walks, and even glacial moraines and rock glaciers to explore.

A Spectacular Wildlife Habitat

Alpine meadows full of wildflowers, pristine valleys, and rocky cirques offer excellent habitats in this region for Columbian ground squirrels, marmots, bighorn sheep, deer, elk, and both black and grizzly bears. So beware! The abundance of prey and wild berries in these areas are a definite attraction for grizzly bears, and from time to time trails in the region are closed due to grizzly activity.

Fire at the Pass

Two major forest fires have ravaged the pass in the past hundred years. Almost all of the mature spruce and fir in the Highwood Pass was burned in the great fires of 1919 and 1939. The Phillips fire of 1939 was massive. It started in the Upper Elk Valley of British Columbia, moved across the

Continental Divide, and ravaged everything in its path. Only trees in the Misty Basin were spared from this fire, which was finally extinguished by a heavy three-day rain.

The Entry to Highwood Pass

Elpoca and Gap Mountains mark the southern end of the Opal Range. Gap Mountain separates the peaks of the Opal Range from those of the Elk Range. The spectacular view shown above is from the Kananaskis Lakes Trail near the entrance to the North Interlakes day use area.

Elpoca Mountain 3029 m

George Pocaterra has two mountains, a ridge, a creek, and a hydroelectric dam named in his honour. Elpoca is one of those two mountains, and the name is a peculiar combination of the names Elbow Lake and Pocaterra. See if you can figure it out!

First ascent of Elpoca Mountain

Pocaterra Ridge

was in 1960 by G.D. Elliot, H. Kirby, and P.S. Scribens. From Elbow Lake they ascended scree slopes and slabs to a ridge, which they followed north to the true summit in a little over two hours.

Gap Mountain 2675 m

This name is a descriptive one. As mentioned, Gap Mountain separates the peaks of the Opal Range from those of the Elk Range. The first recorded ascent was a solo in August 1977 by J. Mitchell.

Pocaterra Ridge 2667 m

Pocaterra Ridge consists of four identifiable summits. Those shown above are the two closest to the Highwood Pass parking lot, viewed from the interpretive trail to the Highwood Pass Meadows. The highest summit of the ridge (2667 m) is the peak at centre-left in the panorama.

George Pocaterra: A Kananaskis Legend

"All seemed peaceful and serene until I saw the horseman approaching. The rider was McKenzie, an Australian, the recently appointed forest ranger of the Kananaskis Country, and he very decidedly got off on the wrong foot with Pocaterra. 'Are you the guide of this party?' he asked. Pocaterra stared at him with all the anger of an old-timer who is questioned by a newcomer. 'Guide?' he said. 'I don't know about that, but I am George Pocaterra. Those are my coal claims down there; that ridge between the two mountains and this creek was named after me by the survey. And this is a private party."

R.M. Patterson, recalling a
Pocaterra moment

Pocaterra Ridge

George Pocaterra circa 1911, on his favourite horse, Don

If ever there was a true hero of Kananaskis Country, it was George Pocaterra. Born in Rocchette, Italy, in 1883, he had a privileged upbringing, attending the University of Berne in Switzerland. He arrived in Canada in 1903 with $3.75 in his pocket and began homesteading in 1904 with his brother on the banks of the Highwood River, on what would later become a dude ranch called the Buffalo Head Ranch.

It wasn't long before Pocaterra began a lifelong friendship with the Stoney Indians. One, named Three Buffalo Bulls, took him into his family, and Pocaterra became a blood brother to his son Spotted Wolf (whom Pocaterra referred to as Paul Amos).

The Stoney thought Pocaterra was quite a character. They referred to the creek that bears his name today as *Wasiju Wachi tusin ta Waptan ze*. This name requires some explanation. It translates literally as crazy, mischievous, or foolish, referring to Pocaterra's actions while spending time with the Stoney. "Crazy white man" was because he was not all there, and "foolish" was because he misinterpreted many Stoney customs. *Wasiju Wachi tusin ze Ipabin Oke Na Ze* was the Stoney name given to the Pocaterra Ridge region of Highwood Pass where Pocaterra mined for coal.

It was Three Buffalo Bulls who introduced him to the Kananaskis Lakes. Pocaterra called this area "the most beautiful mountain scenery in the world." Here, along with his Stoney friends, he ran traplines and prospected in the region for gypsum,

George Pocaterra circa 1950, in the Ghost River country after his return from Italy

salt deposits and coal.

Pocaterra sold Buffalo Head Ranch to R.M. Patterson in 1933 and returned to Italy, where he met Canadian opera star Norma Piper. They were married in 1936 and returned together to Canada at the beginning of the Second World War to develop a ranch along the Ghost River. Pocaterra had returned to the land and the life he loved, but the Kananaskis Valley had changed and would never be the same again.

Returning to the Kananaskis Lakes in 1963, Pocaterra was saddened by the spoiling of the scenery with the building of the power dam. "The drowning of the marvelously beautiful islands and exquisitely curving beaches, the cutting down of centuries-old trees, and the drying up of the falls between the two lakes" was more than George Pocaterra could bear. Little did he realize that this power plant would later bear his name, as would a mountain ridge, two peaks, and a creek. George Pocaterra died at the age of 89 in March 1972.

Mount Rae 3225 m

Mount Rae, the highest peak east of the Kananaskis Trail, was named by James Hector in honour of the Arctic explorer Dr. John Rae. The peak is high enough to be viewed on the western skyline even from Calgary.

Rae (1813–1893) was one of the greatest Arctic explorers, and many historians believe he was the true discoverer of the Northwest Passage. Rae was born in the Orkney Islands off the north coast of Scotland. He graduated from Edinburgh University as a qualified surgeon and was only 20 years old when appointed surgeon to a Hudson's Bay Company ship in 1833.

Rae glacier on the northwest side of the mountain is the true source of the Elbow River and of most of Calgary's drinking water. It has been re-

ceding at an alarming rate over the past twenty-five years.

G. Langille and E.H.J. Smyth made the first recorded ascent of the peak in 1950, from the south col and then the south ridge to the summit in six and a half hours. They reported a cairn on the summit, but extensive searching found no record left by the builders.

Franklin's First and Second Expeditions

John Rae gave over thirty years of his life to exploring and documenting the northern edge of North America. He was also part of four expeditions aimed at determining the fate of the last Franklin expedition.

Mt. Rae

John Franklin's First Expedition to the Canadian Arctic (1819–1821) resulted in eleven deaths. His own account of the expedition included stories of murder, starvation, and even cannibalism—sensational elements that caused the British public to overlook Franklin's inexperience and bad judgment as contributing factors to their misfortune.

Franklin's Second Overland Expedition (1825–1827) began at Great Slave Lake and then travelled northwest down the Mackenzie River to the Beaufort Sea. Two of his parties explored much of the northern coast of Alaska as well as eastward to the Coppermine River. On this expedition they travelled over 2,000 miles without suffering any casualties.

Mount Rae looks magnificent from Highwood Ridge, immediately above the Highwood Pass parking lot.

The Ill-fated Last Expedition

Franklin's last expedition (1845-1847) in search of the coveted Northwest Passage would prove tragic. He set out in two ships, the *Erebus* and the *Terror*, with a crew of 133 men. A supply ship, the *Baretto Junior*, accompanied them to the coast of Greenland, where supplies were transferred. The two ships with 129 remaining men sailed into the ice-choked waters of the Davis Strait, never to be seen again.

Historians tell us the expedition spent the first winter on Beechey Island, and the second winter off the coast of King William Island, where Franklin died on June 11, 1847. They spent another winter frozen in before the 105 survivors abandoned the ships. Little is known from this point on, but tradition tells us that most died on King William Island and only a handful made it to the mainland before dying.

Rae and the Search for Franklin

During his explorations Rae covered over 36,000 kilometres, many on foot or by snowshoe. His success in the cruel climate of the north can be attributed to his means of survival, his learning and adopting of the ways of the Inuit, his fine leadership qualities and his exceptional strength. He regarded these Arctic journeys as nothing more than part of his job. In a letter he wrote to R.H. Major in 1875, Rae stated, "We of the Hudson's Bay Company thought very little of our Arctic work. For my own part at least, I thought no more of it than any other journey."

It was Rae's final expedition that caused the greatest uproar. On this final expedition of 1853–54 he found evidence among the Pelly Bay Inuit that allowed him to reconstruct the Franklin tragedy. His conclusions caused a furor in England.

Evidence of Cannibalism

Rae returned to England in 1854 with startling evidence of the demise of the Franklin crew. He brought back spoons, knives, forks, and trays, but the aspect of his report that caused repulsion was the evidence of cannibalism. Rae wrote, "From the mutilated state of many of the corpses and the contents of the kettles, it is evident that our wretched countrymen had been driven to the last resort—cannibalism—as a means of prolonging existence." The British public and most of the British Admiralty refused to believe such accusations. Most people felt that eating the remains of another human being was so abhorrent that it was inconceivable that British sailors of military discipline would resort to such action. Rae became an object of disrespect and was even ridiculed by Charles Dickens, who emphatically stated, "British sailors would never do such a thing!" Dickens attacked Rae's story as being secondhand, and even went so far as to blame the Inuit for the murder of the members of the Franklin Expedition.

The pathological evidence gathered by Dr. Owen Beattie in 1986 finally vindicated Dr. Rae.

Vindication of Dr. John Rae, and Lead Poisoning

The first conclusive evidence that cannibalism occurred on the Franklin Expedition came from the pathological work of Dr. Owen Beattie of the University of Alberta in 1981, 1982 and 1984 on King William Island. In 1986 his research team returned to another site on Beechey Island, where they conducted two more autopsies. In all cases, although they found medical problems with the dead men, they found no direct evidence as to the cause of their deaths or to the demise of the Franklin Expedition. But they did find evidence of cannibalism. They observed cut marks on 92 bones that could only have been made by a sharp blade, and other evidence that human flesh had been cooked.

Beattie's research team conducted complete autopsies on three intact corpses of members of the Franklin Expedition and reported some startling discoveries. They found levels of lead in human hair samples ranging from 138 ppm to as high as 657 ppm. These levels are over twenty times higher than the accepted levels in a standard human sample.

Dr. John Rae

How could levels of lead in these tissue samples be so high? At the time of the Franklin Expedition tinned preserved food was a relatively recent innovation. The seams of tin cans and the tops and bottoms were sealed with solder that consisted of more than 90 per cent lead. The acidic nature of the canned food caused lead to become incorporated into the food the sailors were eating. The expedition was supplied with over eight thousand such cans of preserved food.

Although lead poisoning did not lead to the demise of the Franklin Expedition, it must have played a role in its failure. Sustained blood levels of 0.05 mg support a diagnosis of lead poisoning. Symptoms of lead poisoning are weight loss, loss of energy, convulsions and permanent damage to the central nervous system, producing neurotic or erratic behavior. These are not conditions conducive to survival under extreme Arctic conditions.

The Battles of Heligoland Bight and Dogger Bank

These two battles, although of minor importance in the whole scheme of things, are recounted here because of their connection to Mounts Arethusa and Tyrwhitt, two peaks in the Highwood Pass region. Here again is an example of the power A.O. Wheeler had in the naming of peaks — choosing to name them after warships and admirals that had little if anything to do with Kananaskis history.

Heligoland Bight
August 28, 1914

The first naval battle of World War I between the two great naval powers, Great Britain's Grand Fleet and Germany's High Seas Fleet, was the Battle of Heligoland Bight in August 1914. A British plan to attack German patrols in the Heligoland Bight off the northwest coast of Germany was to be undertaken by the Royal Navy's Harwich

Mt. Arethusa

Mount Arethusa from the Highwood Pass day use area

January 23, 1915. Their intent was a raiding mission of British patrols off the northeast coast of Britain at the Dogger Bank. The German surprise attack did not materialize, due to superior British intelligence. Instead, it was the German fleet that was ambushed by Tyrwhitt and Beatty's cruisers. Von Hipper was forced to turn and head for home waters with the faster British fleet in close pursuit.

In the running battle, the German cruiser *Blucher* was severely damaged by the *Arethusa*. After receiving 50 salvos and two torpedo hits, the *Blucher* capsized, with her side jutting out of the water. Men standing on the sinking hull began diving into the waters of the North Sea hoping for rescue. Only 123 men were rescued from a crew of 1,077 officers and men.

Unfortunately, botched British communications by Rear Admiral Arthur Moore resulted in the escape of the rest of the German fleet, and the Grand Fleet thus lost an excellent opportunity to destroy four German battle cruisers. Beatty's wrath resulted in the removal of Moore from command.

Force under the command of Sir Reginald Tyrwhitt. His squadron, consisting of his flagship HMS *Arethusa* along with the cruiser Fearless and two flotillas of destroyers, quickly dispatched two German torpedo boats, but the arrival of additional German cruisers resulted in an outgunned British naval force.

Tyrwhitt's force was being heavily pounded and the *Arethusa* was in serious trouble when Admiral Beatty, displaying his characteristic reckless abandon, charged headlong into the battle. Beatty's First Battlecruiser Squadron saved Tyrwhitt's flotilla, sinking three German cruisers and heavily damaging three others. Germany lost more than 1,000 sailors, in comparison to one light cruiser and less than 50 casualties on the side of the Royal Navy. This action also brought considerably fame and glory to Beatty. The crippled *Arethusa* limped home to be quickly repaired and take part in the Battle of Dogger Bank.

Dogger Bank
January 24, 1915

This incident began when the German First Scouting Group under the command of Rear Admiral Franz von Hipper left Germany on the night of

Mount Arethusa
2912 m

Seven ships of the Royal Navy have carried the name *Arethusa,* but the mountain in Kananaskis was named for the gallant *Arethusa* that was commanded by Commodore Sir Reginald Tyrwhitt. as mentioned above, his ship took part in the Battles of Heligoland Bight and Dogger Bank during World War I. In Greek mythology, Arethusa was a woodland nymph, which may be the origin of the name of the battleship, but not of the mountain.

W.D. Grant and A. Larson scrambled up the southeast ridge in June 1971, to claim first ascent of the peak.

In an encounter with two German cruisers at the Battle of Heligoland

Bight on August 28, 1914, three newly-fitted guns on the *Arethusa* jammed, and a fourth was put out of commission when its magazine was hit. With one remaining gun, the *Arethusa* continued to fight, but was seriously damaged. Flooding of her main boiler reduced her speed to 10 knots, and it was by no means certain that she could be towed home. However, the gallant *Arethusa* did make it to her home port, was refitted, and was then responsible for the sinking of the German cruiser *Blucher* at the Battle of Dogger Bank in January 1915.

Ode to the Arethusa

The British Admiralty acclaimed the actions of the *Arethusa* and instructed that a brass plate engraved with the following verse be affixed to a conspicuous place on her deck. It reads:

*Come all ye jolly Sailors bold,
whose hearts are cast in honour's mold
    While English glory I unfold,
    Huzza for the 'Arethusa'.
Her men are staunch to their favorite launch.
And when the foe shall meet our
    fire, sooner than strike,
We'll all expire on board of the
    'Arethusa'.
And now we've driven the foe
    ashore, never to fight with
    Britons more.
Let each fill his glass, to his
    favourite lass;
A health to our captain and officers true, and all that belong to
    the jovial crew,
    On board of the 'Arethusa'.*

The Misty Range

Storm Mtn.

The Misty Range and its individual peaks were named by Dr. George Mercer Dawson during his geological trip through Alberta and British Columbia in 1884. Dawson experienced rainstorms during his geological exploration of the region, and the whole range has a propensity for attracting dreadful weather.

Storm Mountain
3092 m

Storm Mountain was named by Dr. Dawson for the storm clouds that seemed to forever swirl about its summit. G. Langille and E.H.J. Smyth recorded the first ascent of the mountain in 1971. They followed the narrow south ridge northward to the summit.

There are two arches visible from the Kananaskis Trail in the Highwood Pass region. One is on the southeast

Storm Mountain from the Highwood Pass day use area

Mist Mtn.

Mt. Lipsett

Highwood Ridge

Unnamed

Mist Mountain and Mount Lipsett (top)

Highwood Ridge (above)

ridge of Mt. Tyrwhitt, and the other is a beautiful arch on the shoulder of Storm Mountain. Arches such as these are produced by the forces of erosion on exposed, thin ridges. Over millions of years, weak layers of rock in the ridge collapse, leaving a hole or window in the ridge.

Mist Mountain 3142 m

Major General Louis J. Lipsett

Dawson also named Mist Mountain in 1884, en route to the Sheep River region via Misty Basin. Some think he named the mountain not for the atrocious weather around the peak but for the clouds of mist that arise from small hot springs near its southeast base when the temperature drops to the freezing point. The hot springs, located in a remote part of Mist Creek Valley, are rumoured to be warm enough to take a dip in, even in the cooler months of the year. Two creeks that arise in the Misty Range—Storm and Mist creeks— converge in the valley to join the Highwood River.

E.H.J. Smyth and G. Langille reached the summit of Mist Mountain in October 1948 via its southeast ridge, and since no cairn was found, assumed they had made a first ascent. Further inquiry revealed that first ascent of this mountain had occurred in 1946 by the three Blayney Brothers along with D. King via the easy southeast ridge, from the Highwood Valley.

Mount Lipsett 2580 m

This mountain commemorates Major General Louis J. Lipsett, Commander of the 1st Canadian Division at the battles of Vimy Ridge and the Somme during World War I. Later in the war Lipsett was promoted to commander of the Third Army of the Canadian Expeditionary Corps.

Highwood Ridge 2708 m

As you approach Highwood Pass, just south of the Elbow Lake day use area on the Kananaskis Trail, the summit of Highwood Ridge comes into view. This is the same summit that looms over the Highwood Pass parking lot

Mt. Tyrwhitt

and day use area, extending as a long straight ridge for approximately 5 kilometres before it drops off the southeastern end near Mt. Lipsett.

Mount Tyrwhitt 2874 m

Mount Tyrwhitt can be reached by a hiking trail to Pocaterra Cirque and Little Highwood Pass through spectacular meadows containing alpine larch. The peak was named in honour of Sir Reginald Tyrwhitt (1870-1951), commander of the Royal Navy's Harwich Force in World War I. The major function of Tyrwhitt's force was to counter the regular attacks to the east coast of Britain by German battle cruisers.

Tyrwhitt displayed great initiative and courage in commanding his force of light cruisers and destroyers, which was used quite extensively and suffered heavy losses early in the war. He was a strong advocate of naval aviation and his ships launched many seaplane raids against German land targets. His force was the first into action at the Battle of Heligoland Bight in 1914, where his flagship HMS *Arethusa* suffered heavy damage. He also took part in the Battle of Dogger Bank. In the postwar period he was promoted, in 1934, to the rank of Ad-

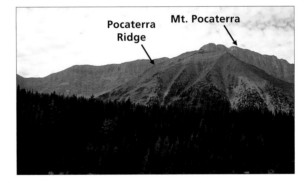

Pocaterra Ridge   Mt. Pocaterra

miral of the Fleet. His greatest regret was having had to miss the Battle of Jutland in 1916 due to orders from the admiralty.

The Boundary Commission made the first ascent of the mountain in 1915 and set up a camera station on its summit.

Mount Pocaterra 2934 m

A spectacular exposed ridge connects Mt. Pocaterra (the name is unofficial) to Mt. Tyrwhitt to the southeast. The name of the mountain is yet another honour bestowed on George Pocaterra, and from the Kananaskis Trail the peak can just be seen poking its head above the fourth summit of Pocaterra Ridge

Mount Tyrwhitt (top)

Pocaterra Ridge and Mount Pocaterra (above)

Sir Reginald Tyrwhitt

The Smith-Dorrien Valley

The Smith-Dorrien Drainage System

Peaks of the Kananaskis Range

The Smith-Dorrien Valley is bounded on the north by the peaks of the Kananaskis Range and on the south by the peaks of the Spray Range, commonly referred to as The British Military Group. The Smith-Dorrien/Spray Lakes Trail (Hwy. 742) provides quick access to these peaks, but do be prepared for dust and flying stones on this gravel road.

A major thrust fault called the Bourgeau Thrust formed the Smith-Dorrien Valley millions of years ago. The valley was then sculpted by the Burstall Glacier, which descended from the Continental Divide down the Burstall Creek Valley. One arm of the glacier descended toward Spray Lakes, while another moved toward the Kananaskis Lakes. The Haig Icefield, a remnant of this glacier, still exists in the center of these peaks. Mud Lake, at an elevation of 1908 meters, is at the height of the pass that separates the Smuts Creek drainage (flowing into Spray Lakes) from the Smith-Dorrien Creek drainage system (flowing to the Kananaskis Lakes).

Archaeological excavations during construction of the Smith-Dorrien section of the trail unearthed numerous historical sites dating back thousands of years. It is evident from the finds at these sites that both the Spray and Smith-Dorrien valleys were major thoroughfares for hunter-gatherers.

Peaks of the Kananaskis Range

Mount Kent 2635 m

Mount Kent is a minor peak of the Kananaskis Range — nothing more than a long ridge culminating in a low summit. Together, the ridge and summit guard the southern entrance into the Smith-Dorrien drainage system. The peak is best viewed from the Sawmill day use area on the Smith-Dorrien/Spray Trail, where it looms directly above you. It was named to honour HMS *Kent*, an armoured cruiser built in 1903. *Kent* was equipped with fourteen 6-inch guns and had a maximum speed of 24 knots. Under the command of Captain J.D. Allen, she took part in the Battle of the Falklands in 1915.

Mt. Kent

HMS Kent at the Falklands

At the Falklands in 1915, HMS *Kent* took a pounding in a fierce battle with the German cruiser *Nurnberg*. However, even after being hit 38 times, she was able to dispatch the German cruiser. The *Kent* suffered sixteen casualties; one of them, a seaman named Kelly, had both his legs blown off before becoming unconscious and slowly dying.

Covered with salvos, the German ship almost appeared to melt away before the eyes of the British sailors. Her whole forepart was glowing from the heat of internal fires, but still she did not surrender. Again she was pounded by salvos from the *Kent*, and finally, after a fight as gallant as any in naval history, struck her colours. All but seven of the *Nurnberg* crew perished.

Captain Allan was very near to losing his own ship in this battle when a shell burst within a gun port, shooting flames into the ammunition passage. Only Sergeant Charles Mayes' quick

action of flooding this compartment saved the *Kent* from disaster. Mayes was rewarded for his heroism with the Medal for Conspicuous Gallantry. The *Kent* was with *Glasgow* when they found and finally sank the *Dresden* in the Bay of Juan Fernandez off the coast of Chile, finally bringing the Battle of the Falklands to an end.

Mount Chester 3054 m

Mount Chester was named in honour of HMS *Chester*, a light cruiser attached to the 4th Battlecruiser Squadron at the Battle of Jutland. The mountain towers over the beautiful alpine Chester Lake, which is situated in a meadow full of alpine wildflowers and surrounded by alpine larch. The whole valley invites exploration.

The first recorded ascent of Mt. Chester was in 1973 by P. Vermeulen and J. and P. deKrasinski via the southwest slopes in 3 3/4 hours. A cairn was present on the summit, with no record of ascent, however. Today, Mt. Chester is one of the most popular scrambles of peaks over 3000 metres.

At the Battle of Jutland, only a miracle saved HMS *Chester* from total destruction. She was steaming at full speed when she encountered German

Mount Kent, viewed from James Walker Creek, 1.5 km west of the Sawmill day use area on the Smith-Dorrien/ Spray Trail

109

Scouting Group II and was immediately fired upon by four cruisers. The third and fourth German salvos destroyed all fire control communications and caused heavy casualties to *Chester's* gun crews. In only nineteen minutes of battle, the cruiser was hit seventeen times, with 77 men killed and 39 injured. This devastating

Chester Lake beneath the slopes of Mt. Chester

pounding left unspeakable human carnage. Sub-Lieutenant Phipps-Hornby found himself desensitized to all the death around him on the *Chester*. He calmly sat eating his lunch as the cook told him how he found his mate lying dead with the top of his head neatly sliced off "just as you might slice off the top of a boiled egg." Only skilful maneuvering by Captain Robert N. Lawson saved the *Chester* from certain doom.

Mount Galatea 3185 m

Mount Galatea is the highest peak in the Kananaskis range. The peak was named for the light battle cruiser

HMS *Galatea*, which was commanded by Commodore E.S. Alexander-Sinclair at the Battle of Jutland. Fleeting glimpses of Mt. Galatea may be obtained from the Kananaskis Trail, but better views exist on the Smith-Dorrien/Spray Trail or the Watridge Logging road near Mount Engadine Lodge.

The first ascent of Mt. Galatea was by Katie Gardiner and Walter Feuz in 1930. From a fly camp pitched in a valley south of the peak, they began an ascent of the south face on hard snow and in a mist. They were forced to wait out the heavy mist under a rock shelter for about two hours, after which they had no trouble reaching the summit in a little over 6 1/2 hours. Katie wrote, "The view from the top of Galatea was very extensive, but we were not able to enjoy it for very long as a nasty electrical hailstorm commenced, which stung us badly. Walter hurried me off to a more sheltered spot."

The two concluded their climbing trip to the Kananaskis region with first ascents of Mounts Sarrail, Foch, Cordonnier, Warrior, Lyautey, and Bogart, in what must be regarded as one of the greatest climbing trips in the history of the Kananaskis. And just for the fun of it, they also made the second ascent of Mt. Joffre to cap off a terrific summer of climbing!

First Blood at Jutland

The *Galatea* had the distinction of being the first battle cruiser in the Battle of Jutland to encounter and engage the enemy. At precisely 2:15 P.M. on May 31, 1916, the *Galatea*, while on reconnaissance duty, hoisted the general flag signal "Enemy in sight".

At 15,000 yards the German cruiser *Elbing* scored the first hit in the Battle of Jutland when one of her shells smashed through the bridge of the *Galatea*. Fortunately it failed to explode, and only caused minor damage. *Galatea* exchanged ineffectual fire with the German cruiser, and the Battle of Jutland had begun. The Royal Navy made many mistakes in this battle, and the first was made by *Galatea* in pursuing the German cruisers rather than maintaining her reconnaissance duty. This deprived Admiral Jellicoe of much-needed accurate intelligence of the situation at a critical moment of the battle.

We can only wonder whether Katie or Walter knew that the mountain they had just climbed in 1930 was named after the British ship that fired the first salvos in the greatest naval battle of the First World War.

The Tower 3117 m

The Tower lies 1 1/2 km east-south-east of Mt. Engadine, and is best viewed from the Mount Shark access road in the Smith-Dorrien Valley. According to Boles, Kruszyna and Putnam (1979) the peak was first ascended in June 1957 by F.W. Crickard, R. Higgins and Hans Gmoser via the north ridge. However, the picture of 'The Tower' by Higgins in the 1958 edition of the Canadian Alpine Journal, which describes the climb, portrays the The Fortress and not The Tower.

Mount Engadine 2970 m

Mount Engadine was named in honor of HMS *Engadine*, the first ship to carry and deploy seaplanes during World War I, at the Battle of Jutland. Early on that fateful day in June 1916, Admiral Beatty ordered Captain C.G. Robinson of the *Engadine* to send up a seaplane to scout the enemy's position. The plane was flown by Lieutenant F.J. Rutland (also know as Rutland of Jutland!). After sighting the German fleet, counting the ships and noting their course, Rutland sent the information on wireless telegraphy from the seaplane to Beatty, thereby

Mt. Galatea

completing the first-ever aerial reconnaissance of a naval battle.

Low cloud necessitated that Rutland fly at an altitude of 900 feet. When he sighted enemy cruisers, they opened fire on his scouting plane with every gun they could bear. Rutland narrowly avoided destruction, but a broken carburetor forced an early landing after barely half an hour

The south slope of Mount Galatea from Three Lakes Valley was the ascent route of the first party in 1930.

The Tower

aloft. The resourceful Rutland succeeded in repairing the defect, but the seaplane was ordered to be hoisted aboard the *Engadine*, thus ending the first use of a heavier-than-air seaplane in a naval battle.

The *Engadine* and Lieutenant Rutland were not finished performing their acts of heroism. Early in the morning of June 1, 120 miles northwest of Jutland, the *Engadine* was attempting to tow the crippled HMS *Warrior* to the safety of their home port when worsening sea conditions caused the *Warrior* to lose her battle

The Tower from Watridge Logging road, 2 km from the junction with Smith-Dorrien/ Spray Trail

Mt. Engadine

View of Mount Engadine from the Mount Shark helipad on the Watridge Logging road, 3.4 km from the Smith-Dorrien/Spray Trail junction

with the North Sea. Despite gale force winds and gigantic waves, the *Engadine* was able to rescue the remaining 650 surviving crew members of the *Warrior* before the armoured cruiser sank beneath the North Sea. During the transfer of survivors from the *Warrior* to the *Engadine*, Rutland jumped into the icy waters of the North Sea in order to save a wounded crewman who had fallen overboard. This selfless act of heroism added the Albert Medal to the Distinguished Service Order that he was awarded for his reconnaissance flight earlier that day.

Mount Buller 2805 m

Mount Buller is directly above the east shore of Spray Lake, near the south end of the lake. It is one of the few peaks in Kananaskis Country that is named in recognition of a Canadian who served in the First World War. In this case, the peak was named in 1922 for Lieutenant Colonel H.C. Buller (1882–1916). Buller was an advisor to the Governor General from 1911 to 1914, before joining Princess Patricia's Canadian Light Infantry. In 1915 he received the Distinguished Service Award, and was later killed in action near Zillebeke.

Mt. Buller

Mount Buller, also as seen from the Mount Shark helipad

The first ascent of Mt. Buller occurred in June 1956, when B. Fraser, M. Hicks, and J. Gorrill ascended open slopes from the Spray River fire road to the col southwest of the peak. From there, they scrambled over talus, slabs, and a short ridge to the summit.

On April 18, 1989, a fatal accident occurred here when a young man attempting to solo the mountain was hit by large boulders from a rock avalanche in a gully on the southwest side of the mountain.

Mount Warspite 2850 m

This mountain was named in honour of HMS *Warspite*, which is a time-honoured name of the Royal Navy. Of the several warships that have carried the name, the first was a 36-gun ship built in 1596 during the reign of Queen Elizabeth I, while the most recent was a Royal Navy nuclear submarine. The battle cruiser after which this mountain was named was a member of the Queen Elizabeth class of battleships, which was the pinnacle of dreadnought technology—powerful, fast, and battle-worthy.

HMS *Warspite* was a member of the Fifth Battle Squadron of fast battleships, under the command of Captain E.M. Phillpotts at Jutland. She was armed with eight 15-inch guns, fourteen 6-inch guns, and four submerged torpedo tubes. Protected by a massive 13-inch armour belt, she had a maximum speed of 24 knots.

Warspite was notorious for getting herself into trouble. At Jutland, heavy into battle, she was hit at least thirteen times by German salvos, while suffering only thirteen casualties. Remarkably, she did not sink, but her steering jammed. This forced her to circle not once but twice in front of the German line as six German warships used her for target practice with their concentrated fire. Her funnels had so many shell holes, they looked like colanders. Turrets were hit and cordite fires in the ammunition rooms resulted in many grisly casualties. Fires were burning in seven different areas of the ship. Men with clothes burned off and charred skin screamed to be put out of their misery. A Catholic priest dragged many of these men from this inferno to safety and won the Distinguished Service Award for his bravery. The *Warspite* lay in this helpless predicament for over 30 minutes, becoming a sitting duck. Despite having over 150 holes blasted into her hull, however, she managed to survive.

The *Warspite* seemed to live a charmed life and survived to fight in World War II, when she became known as 'The Old Lady'. In that war, this survivor of Jutland helped turn the scales of battle for the Allied armies at Salerno, even though she barely survived bombing raids and striking a mine in the North Sea later in the war. Her career finally ended in 1947 when she broke her tow on the way to the wreckers and ran aground on the coast of Cornwall. Scraps of her hull are still salvaged as souvenirs when they wash ashore.

B. Fraser, J. Gorrill, and M. Hicks were, unwittingly, the first to climb Mt. Warspite via its northeast ridge in 1956. They originally thought they had climbed Mt. Black Prince! Almost twenty years later, in 1975, Peter Vermeulen discovered their mistake when he found their Kodak film canister in the summit cairn on Mt. Warspite after his party assumed they had made the first ascent of the peak.

Mount Black Prince
2932 m

This mountain was named in honor of HMS *Black Prince*, a warship of the First Battle Cruiser Squadron at the Battle of Jutland, commanded by Captain Thomas P. Bonham.

What is the origin of this unusual name? The Black Prince was the eldest son of King Edward III of England, who fought against the French in the Hundred Years war. His name referred to the black suit of armour he wore into battle. The Black Prince died in 1376 at the age of 46, before he could assume the throne, but not before fathering the future king of England, Richard II.

The first ascent of Mt. Black Prince was in August 1975 by G. Kinnear and K. Myhre. Not content with that, the two continued southeast and traversed Unnamed (2880 m), Mt. Warspite, Unnamed (2790 m), Mt. Invincible and finally Mt. Indefatigable. The Unnamed peaks were also first ascents.

HMS *Black Prince* had been lost for most of the night at the Battle of Jutland in 1916, and when she finally rejoined the rest of her squadron just after midnight on June 1, met a fearful end. She was under the constant fire of five German battleships and began burning like a gigantic funeral pyre. After being under fire for only about four minutes, she blew up in what Admiral Scheer of the German High Seas Fleet called a "grand but terrible sight." There were no survivors among the 1,026 able seamen and officers.

Mount Warspite from the Peninsula day use area

Mount Black Prince from the Smith-Dorrien/Spray Trail, 2 km west of the Black Prince day use area

Peaks of the British Military Group

Mt. Murray

Mt. Cegnfs

The beautiful pyramidal shape of Mount Murray

The peaks in this region, sometimes referred to as the British Military Group, are spectacular. They occupy about 13 km of the Great Divide between the South Kananaskis and Palliser passes. Technically, they belong to the Spray Range. The principle summits are in the center of the group around the Haig Glacier, and are dominated by Mount Sir Douglas, named after Field Marshal Sir Douglas Haig. Wheeler's Boundary Commission report states that other peaks, "not quite so lofty, have been named after commanders in the British army and navy who have made for themselves great war records in the service of the Empire."

The British Military Group is drained by the Spray River on the north, by the Kananaskis River on the east, and by the Palliser River on the west. The Boundary Commission in 1916 made first ascents of some of these peaks, but most of the

General Sir A.J. Murray

major summits were not climbed until the 1920s.

Mount Murray 3023 m

Mount Murray is an impressive peak just south of the Smith-Dorrien/Spray Trail in the British Military Group. The peak was named for General Sir A.J. Murray, Chief of the Imperial General Staff in 1915 and commanding general of the forces in Egypt in 1916-1917. Why does General Murray warrant having a major peak named after him? Many other possible names with some local historical relevance were overlooked by the Boundary Commission in favour of Mt. Murray.

In the summer of 1968, W. Lyons, W. Saville, D. Judd, T. Cline and two others from the YMCA Wilderness Camp #1 Group made the first ascent of Mt. Murray along the northwest spur and then followed the southeast ridge to the summit.

Cegnfs, the minor peak about 1 1/4 km north of Mt. Murray, is a subsidiary summit. Its unusual name is comprised of letters from the names of the first summit party in August 1972: C. Findlay, P. Findlay, M. Gould, J. Noaks, P. Poole and B. Schiesser.

Mount French 3234 m

John Denton Pinkstone French, the son of Captain William French and Margaret Eccles, was born in Ripple, Kent in 1852. He served with the 19th Hussars in the Sudan (1884-85) and was a cavalry commander in South Africa during the Boer War (1889-1901).

French was appointed Chief of the Imperial Staff in 1911 and served as the first commander of the British Expeditionary Force on the Western Front during WW I, a position for which many said he was temperamentally unsuited. Haig likened his demeanor to "the opening of a soda-bottle, all froth and bubble, without the ability to think clearly and come to a reasoned conclusion." At one point French became so depressed about the prospects of success that his only concern was the safety of his own troops, even at the expense of his allies.

French became very pessimistic about the tactics of the war, and pressure had to be applied in order to persuade him to take part in the first offensive at the Marne. After bitter disagreements, he resigned in December 1915, and Haig replaced him as leader of the British Expeditionary Force. Thereafter he became commander of the British home forces and was finally rewarded with the post of Lord Lieutenant of Ireland from 1918 to 1921, and was named the First Earl

John French

of Ypres in 1922. Sir John Pinkstone French died in 1925.

In the summer of 1921, the first ascent of Mt. French was made by H.S. Hall Jr., M. Morton Jr., and E. Feuz Jr. From a camp at Maude Brook just above Turbine Canyon, they crossed Haig Glacier to reach the saddle between Mts. Jellicoe and French. To reach the summit they had to cross a very narrow knife-edge, which, Edward Feuz informed the party, had prospects that looked "no good."

Henry Hall described how Feuz "crept gingerly along, sometimes on top and then on the east side, gripping the crest with his

Edward Feuz Jr. on the summit ridge, on first successful ascent of Mt. French in 1921

Mt. Murray   Mt. French   Mt. Robertson

Panorama of Mounts Murray, French, and Robertson

left arm and reaching ahead for a few handholds with his right." After reaching a secure position on the other side of the ridge, Feuz suggested it would make a terrific picture. With his camera in his rucksack and still straddling the ridge, Hall did not take this suggestion with enthusiasm, and thus a great opportunity was lost. It took about forty minutes to complete the last forty yards, the final few feet from the summit being less than twelve inches in width. The ascent was made in less than five hours.

Mount Robertson
3194 m

Mount Robertson is a spectacular-looking peak that lies between Mt. Sir Douglas and Mt. French in the British Military Group. J.H. Hall Jr. described Mt. Robertson as a "crumbling mass and not attractive to climb upon." Even Swiss guide Ernest Feuz was hesitant about the narrow, dangerous nature of its summit ridge.

Sir William Robert Robertson

The mountain was named in honour of Sir William Robert Robertson (1860-1933), a British field marshal and Chief of the Imperial General Staff during World War I.

William Robert Robertson became the first ex-ranking officer to enter the Staff College solely through his own ability and hard work, rather than birthright. Robertson was French's assistant in 1914-15 (see 'Mount French', previous page) and later became his chief of staff. When French was dismissed, Robertson was considered as a successor for the role of commander-in-chief of the British forces in France, but the role went to Haig. Robertson supported Haig in being a leading proponent of the 'Western School', a policy that brought him into direct conflict with Lloyd George, an advocate of the 'Eastern Front'. Robertson passionately believed that only a decisive victory on the Western Front could lead to an end to the war, and that all Eastern Front views were a waste of human effort and lives. In an effort to circumvent the influence of Robertson and many of the army staff, Lloyd George created the Supreme War Council.

This conflict finally came to a head, resulting in the dismissal of Robertson in February 1918, and his assignment to a relatively unimportant home command. His fall from office in the army was strictly political and had nothing to do with his abilities. Indeed, post-war recognition promoted Robertson to field marshal and he received a baronetcy for his distinguished wartime service. Field Marshal Sir William Robert Robertson died in 1933.

Defeat on Robertson

In the summer of 1922, a party consisting of W.F. Gillespie, J.H. Hall Jr., D.J.M. McGeary, A.S. Sibbald, and M.D. Geddes attempted the peak from the col between Mts. Robertson and Sir Douglas. After a late start, they reached the extremely narrow summit ridge and were forced to straddle the ridge with "one foot hanging down into Alberta and the other into British Columbia." After crossing this knife-edge they were still not on the true summit, and were confronted with another long and serrated knife-edge that forced them to retire reluctantly, within a stone's throw of the true summit. A small cairn was built to designate the highest point reached by the party on the ridge.

Robertson Falls

It would be another six years before the virgin peak would feel the tread of human feet on its summit. In the summer of 1928, J.W.A. Hickson and Edward Feuz Jr. were determined to conquer it. Following the extremely narrow southwest ridge, they passed the cairn and point that had repulsed the previous party. The ridge became worse as they progressed along it. Hickson stated that the ridge was "more broken up and blocked by nasty teeth of all sorts of shapes and very friable composition." Belaying was practically impossible, and neither climber enjoyed the exposed position on the ridge. Retracing their steps to the cairn, Feuz spotted a narrow ledge on the right that appeared safer, but that required downclimbing about one hundred feet of steep slabs. By the time they reached this ledge and played out four more rope lengths, Robertson had been conquered. The pointy summit had been reached in a little over six hours, but falling hail and snow left little time for the men to relax and relish their accomplishment. They quickly descended.

Field Marshal Sir Douglas Haig

Mount Sir Douglas (Haig) 3406 m

The imposing Mount Sir Douglas is the highest peak between the Palliser and North Kananaskis Passes. The name honours Field Marshal Sir Douglas Haig (1861–1928), who, during World War I, was commander-in-chief of the British forces in France (1915-1918). Sir Douglas, 1st Earl Haig of Bemersyde, was the son of a wealthy Edinburgh distiller, and owed some of his early advancement to patronage. His marriage to Dorothy Crespigny (maid of honour to both Queen Victoria and Queen Alexandra) gained Haig entry into prestigious court circles. In 1914 he was promoted to full general under the supreme command of General Sir John French. Later, in 1918, he was in

Mt. Sir Douglas

A spectacular view of Mount Sir Douglas from South Burstall Pass

charge of the British advance on the Western Front, which eventually led to victory that same year.

Sir Douglas also led the Allied forces in the First Battle of the Somme, during which they advanced 12 kilometres, suffering 420,000 British and 200,000 French casualties. Haig's tactics were marked by the attrition and 'attack at all costs' mentality. After the war, his tactics and the management of his major campaigns were severely criticized by some, who said he was responsible for the death of millions of brave men who died rather than being called cowards. Military historians have even claimed his tactics were deeply flawed, especially his belief that the cavalry could be sent through the German lines, twenty miles deep, after they had been breached.

Prime Minister David Lloyd George of Britain, reflecting on these tactics after the war, wondered if he should have vetoed them. In his war memoirs, he wrote, "Ought I not to have resigned rather than acquiesce in this slaughter of brave men?" In an interview in 1993, William Brooks, a

private in Haig's army, expressed bitterness at the utter waste and disregard for human life and suffering shown by the military commanders. He ended by saying, "I'd hate to be in their shoes when they face their maker!" Haig is buried beside Sir Walter Scott at Dryburgh Abbey.

The Haig Ultimatum

On April 11, 1918, Haig issued what has become perhaps the most famous military command of World War I. The order was issued to all ranks of the British forces in France and is quoted here in its entirety.

"Three weeks ago to-day the enemy began his terrific attacks upon us on a fifty mile front. His objects are to separate us from the French, to take the Channel Ports, and destroy the British Army. In spite of throwing already 106 divisions into battle, and enduring the most reckless sacrifice of human life, he has yet made little progress towards his goal.

We owe this to the determined fighting and self-sacrifice of our troops. Words fail me to express the admirations, which I feel for the splendid resistance offered by all ranks of our army under most trying circumstances.

Many among us now are tired. To those I would say that victory will belong to the side which holds out the longest. The French army is moving rapidly and in great force to our support.

There is no other course open to us but to fight it out! Every position must be held to the last man: there must be no retirement. With our backs to the wall, and believing in the justice of our cause, each one of us must fight on to the end. The safety of our homes and the freedom of mankind alike depend on the conduct of each one of us at this critical moment."

D. Haig Field Marshal
Order of the Day,
April 11, 1918

First Ascent

During the summer of 1916, Dr. J. W. A. Hickson hired Ed Feuz and a complete outfitter, in order to climb in the mountains of the French and British military group. Although Val Fynn and his party led by Rudolph Aemmer were already in the region, Dr. Hickson was insistent on going in search of first ascents.

Camping just below Palliser Pass, Ed Feuz and the doctor were treated to a magnificent view of Mt. Sir Douglas, and they thought they just might be in luck. The next day they reached the peak's glacier with little difficulty, when Ed asked, "Doctor, would you be willing to climb this mountain today?" "Lead off", Hickson responded. They encountered few problems and were on the summit by 5 P.M. There

was no evidence that anyone else had ever been to the top. They built two cairns, one on each of the twin summits that are clearly visible from Palliser Pass.

That Ridge Will Make a Fine Second Ascent

The next day Hickson and Feuz paid the Aemmer camp a visit, only to be told by Fynn's wife, pointing to a steep ridge, that Rudolph and her husband were climbing Mt. Sir Douglas. Feuz commented on how difficult the route looked, and asked, "I wonder why they didn't go our way, where we went yesterday? We even had a chance to build those two big cairns on top." Mrs. Fynn was dumbfounded, and Feuz responded, "Don't worry, that ridge Rudolph and your husband are on will make a fine second ascent."

As luck would have it, Rudolph and Fynn were thwarted in their attempt on the ridge, and returned to their camp frustrated and weary. They were even more furious to learn that they had already been beaten to the top. When Feuz and Hickson met the Fynn party, who were on their way back to Lake Louise the next morning, not even a hello was said. But Aemmer quickly forgave his best friend for beating him to the top, and recognized the feat in the American Alpine Journal.

Mount Smith-Dorrien
3155 m

Mount Smith-Dorrien is located at the head of the upper Kananaskis River, 1 1/2 km east of Mt. French. The peak was named in honor of General Sir Horace Lockwood Smith-Dorrien (1858-1930), who took part in the Zulu War, the Boer War, and commanded the Second Army during the First World War. The name of the peak honours a man who dared to question his superior officer's orders to

Mt. Smith-Dorrien

Mt. Murray

Cegnfs

Mount Smith-Dorrien from the Smith-Dorrien/Spray Trail, 13.4 km from the Kananaskis Lakes Trail junction

send men into battle against overwhelming odds. He was apalled by the number of casualties and was eventually dismissed for his insubordination.

Smith-Dorrien: The Man Who Disobeyed

General Smith-Dorrien was well-liked by his troops, whom he handled with great respect and sympathy. On the other hand, he had little respect for the abilities of his commander-in-chief, Sir John French. This bad feeling was heartily reciprocated and ultimately led to Smith-Dorrien's dismissal. It is ironic that two men who disliked each other so much should have mountains named in their honour within shouting distance of each other!

Hero worship of Smith-Dorrien began at the Battle of Le Cateau in 1914, when, against overwhelming odds, his exhausted troops would not

General Sir Horace Lockwood Smith-Dorrien

retreat, and held their precarious position. They paid dearly for their victory, suffering over 8,000 casualties, but their heroism saved the British Expeditionary Force from complete destruction.

Smith-Dorrien then led his troops in the 1st Battle of Ypres, where there were an estimated 135,000 German casualties. But then in April 1915, the Germans launched another major offensive, in which deadly chlorine gas was used on the front lines, and the second Battle of Ypres began. Repeatedly ordered into costly and seemingly senseless counterattacks by Sir John French, Smith-Dorrien halted these attacks on his own initiative, thereby saving the lives of thousands of his troops.

When he also recommended the partial abandonment of badly exposed sectors of the Ypres salient against the wishes of French, his fate was sealed. French was not

Commonwealth Pk.

amused with this insubordination, and bearing little affection for his subordinate, removed Smith-Dorrien from his command. Ironically, Smith-Dorrien's replacement, General Sir Herbert Plumer, assessed the situation in much the same manner as his predecessor, and French was ultimately forced to accept most of what Smith-Dorrien had originally proposed. Later, Smith-Dorrien was Governor General of Gibraltar from 1918-23, but was never again to command in the field.

Mount Smith-Dorrien was first ascended from a camp near Turbine Canyon by Mr. and Mrs. Fraser, with E. Feuz Jr., in 1933. The ascent took six hours.

Commonwealth Peak 2775 m

This minor peak was named in March 1979 to commemorate the XI Commonwealth Games that took place in Edmonton from August 3-12, 1978. First ascent of the peak was made in 1970 by C. Locke and L. McKay, via the southeast face, in 3 3/4 hours.

The Pig's Tail 2822 m

Of the first ascent mentioned above, Locke wrote in 1971, "During the summer when my youthful enthusiasm had waned sufficiently, Lloyd and I went exploring. One of the most interesting climbs seemed to be the SE face of a subsidiary peak of Mt. Birdwood, which for reasons known only to ourselves, is named the Pig's Ass." It is apparent that the name has been changed to be more polite: 'The Pig's Tail'.

Mount Burstall 2760 m

Mount Burstall is a minor peak between Burstall and French Creeks. It is connected to Mt. Robertson by a long, high ridge. It is one of the few peaks in Kananaskis Country that is named in honour of a Canadian. Lieutenant General H.E. Burstall (1870–1945) served as an advisor to the Governor General of Canada and later commanded Canadian forces during the First World War. Both the pass and the peak are named in his honour.

In 1972, guide B. Schiesser led the first ascent party up the exposed and

Commonwealth
Peak

Mt. Birdwood

The Pigstail

**Mount Burstall
(left)**

**Mount
Birdwood and
the Pig's Tail
(right)**

crumbly north ridge to the summit in five hours.

Mount Birdwood
3097 m

This spectacular-looking mountain was named in honour of Field Marshal Sir William Riddell Birdwood (1865–1951). Birdwood served in campaigns in India and South Africa before becoming the first commander of the Australian and New Zealand Army Corps (Anzac) in World War I.

Unlike some members of the British command, Birdwood fully appreciated the qualities of his army corps, and they returned this affection. Known as 'Birdy', he was one of the best generals of his day. His four-point order, "Concealment wherever possible; covering fire always; control of fire and control of your men; communications never to be neglected", issued in 1915 to his commanding officers, was considered the epitome of wisdom and good sense.

'Birdy' became Sir William Bird-

wood when he was knighted in 1915, the same year he was promoted to Lieutenant General. He was promoted to Field Marshal in 1925, and his respect for his Anzac troops led to his taking the title 'Baron Birdwood of Anzac and Totnes'. His only disappointment was not becoming governor general of Australia, a post for which he was well-suited.

First ascent of Mt. Birdwood was in July 1922 by C.F. Hogeboom, F.N. Waterman, and R. Aemmer. When they reached a 100-foot-high chimney, wide enough in which to stretch their arms from side to side, they found both walls to be rather smooth, with few handholds. They had reached the crux from which they had to extricate themselves. Here Aemmer showed his resolve. Hogeboom related that "Rudolph got up on Waterman's back, then on his shoulders, and received a shove with the hands as he finally went over the top." The summit was won after 7 1/2 hours of climbing.

Mount Smuts
and the knuckles
of The Fist

Mount Smuts
2938 m

Mount Smuts is another spectacular peak of the Spray Range. In 1926, Rudolph Aemmer led H.S. Crosby, Miss M. Crosby, Miss M. Kennard, and C.A. Willard on the first ascent of the mountain. The ascent took seven hours. Today the peak is considered one of the hardest scrambles in the Rockies, and many rescues have been required.

Mt. Smuts was named to honour Field Marshal Jan Christian Smuts (1870-1950). Born in South Africa, he studied law at Cambridge, only to return to his homeland to support President Paulus Kruger of the South African Republic rather than endorse Cecil Rhodes' dream of a British Africa. During the Boer War, Smuts established himself as a guerrilla leader of exceptional talent. He participated in leading Boer units to victory in 1902 and was present when the surrender was signed that May.

After the South African election of 1907, Smuts became part of Premier Louis Botha's cabinet and was instrumental in writing the constitution when the Union of South Africa was formed in 1910. Smuts became defense minister in Botha's cabinet at the outbreak of the First World War.

Major General Smuts supported the British in the First World War and helped force the surrender of the Germans in East Africa in 1915. He joined the Imperial War Cabinet of Prime Minister David Lloyd George in 1917, and upon the death of Premier Botha in 1919, became Premier of South Africa. He served again in the Second World War with the rank of Field Marshal, and has the distinction of being the only person to sign the peace treaties at the end of both world wars. Smuts was also a leading figure the drafting of the United Nations Charter.

Jan Christian Smuts

Mt. Shark

Mount Shark

Smuts on Mountain Spirituality

The mountain is not something externally sublime; it has a great historic and spiritual meaning for us. It stands for us as the ladder of life. Nay, more; it is the ladder of the soul, and in a curious way the source of religion. From it came the Law; from it came the Gospel in the Sermon on the Mount. We may truly say that the highest religion is the Religion of the Mountain.

Jan Smuts

The Fist 2630 m

Guide Bernie Schiesser first applied this name to the peak in 1973 because it resembled a clenched fist. First ascent did not occur until July 1973, when C. Crosby, D. Grey, G. Kuber, B. McDonald, and M. Toft scrambled up the easy south ridge slopes to the summit.

Mount Shark
2786 m

Mount Shark was named in honor of the HMS *Shark*, a torpedo-boat destroyer and member of the Fourth Destroyer Flotilla at the Battle of Jutland, under the command of Loftus W. Jones.

One of the largest karst springs in North America with an unknown source flows under Mt. Shark, emerging in a torrent on the northeast slopes of the mountain. Mt. Shark is popular today with scramblers. There is no recorded first ascent.

The Gallant Shark

During the Battle of Jutland, Commander Loftus Jones hurled the *Shark* at the numerically superior German force with such ferocity that the enemy was forced to retreat. However, more German battle cruisers appeared, and under a deluge of shells the *Shark*'s main engines were crippled and she became a sitting duck for German target practice. Offered assistance by the captain of HMS

Acasta, Loftus Jones refused, replying, "Tell him to look after himself and not get sunk over us."

The *Shark* was now sinking and shuddering from the impact of every hit. Wounded in the thigh and face and trying to stop the flow of blood, Loftus Jones ordered his coxswain to prepare the lifeboats. One remaining gun was reduced to two crewmen, who maintained a steady fire. When one of them dropped from the loss of blood, Loftus Jones took his place. A moment later, an exploding shell took off his right leg above the knee.

With ebbing strength, and finding that the ship's flag had been shot away, Loftus Jones ordered another flag hoisted to replace it. As

The gallant Captain Loftus W. Jones

the bow of the *Shark* sank, he gave his last order: "Save yourselves!" Survivors lowered him into the water and they floated clear in lifeboats, rafts, and pieces of wreckage. And then the *Shark* was struck amidships by two torpedoes. She sank with colours flying, to which Loftus Jones said, "That's good!" His head then fell forward and his gallant spirit left his body. Eighty-six men went to their watery graves with the *Shark*.

A few weeks later, the body of Commander Loftus Jones, who was awarded a posthumous Victoria Cross, was washed ashore on the coast of Sweden. He was buried in the fashion of the Vikings with a stone at his head and his feet.

HMS Shark

The Spray Lakes Region

The Spray Lakes Drainage System

The magnificent Spray Valley from the summit of Mount Sparrowhawk

A rich valley, agreeably diversi-fied by enamelled meads, mag-nificent forests and lakes, bounded on either side by a suc-cession of picturesque rocks, whose lofty summits, rising in the form of pyramids, lose them-selves in the clouds.

Father de Smet—1845

Today, Father de Smet would hardly recognize the magnifi-cent valley he described in 1845, due to the development of the Spray Reservoir power system. But he would no doubt be pleased that this magnificent valley will be preserved for all time in its present pristine state. On September 20, 2000, Gary Mar, Alberta's environment minister, announced the creation of a new provincial park encompassing the valley. Spray Valley Provincial Park protects 266 square kilometers of wilderness and effectively ends the development of large-scale projects in this ecologically sensitive region.

This was not the case in the early 1920s, when a thirst for hydroelectric power sealed the fate of the many small lakes in the valley. Recognition of the electrical potential of these lakes led to the development of the Spray System in 1951. This system consists of the Canyon Dam at the southwestern end of Spray Lakes and the Three Sisters Dam at its northern end. Together, these two dams create a huge reservoir with a storage cap-acity of nearly 500,000,000 m³. After dropping to the Three Sisters Power Plant, the water passes on its way to the Whiteman Dam and the Spray Power Plant. It joins the Bow River just west of Canmore at the Rundle Power Plant. The total generating power of the Spray System is a huge 155,700 kW of electricity.

Early Explorations in the Valley

The Spray River Valley has a storied past. Recorded history dates back at least to James Sinclair in 1841, and the valley was used as a passageway by nomadic hunters for thousands of years prior to that. It has been witness to hunters, settlers, missionaries, ex-plorers and even spies passing through its pristine landscape.

The valley sits in a spectacular set-ting guarded by the Goat Range on the west and the Kananaskis Range on the east. Captain John Palliser named the Goat Range from the translation of the Stoney name for the sure-footed ungulates that wandered these slopes.

The northern end of the Goat Range lies entirely within Banff Na-tional Park, while the southern end lies within Kananaskis Country, and the southern massif forms the boundary between Banff National Park and Kananaskis Country. Old Goat Mountain (3125 m), an unofficial name, is the highest peak of this range. Mount Nestor lies at the range's extreme southern end.

The mountains of the Kananaskis Range, which lie on the eastern side of the valley, are the same peaks that can be viewed from the Kananaskis Trail (Hwy. 40), but they look entirely different from this aspect.

Although the Spray River Valley had been used by the Stoney and Kootenay Indians for centuries, it was not until 1841 that the first people of European descent visited the valley. James Sinclair (see next section) led a party of 116 emigrants intent on reaching the Oregon Territory from Rocky Mountain House, past Devil's Head to Lake Minnewanka. They eventually crossed the Bow River near present-day Canmore and ascended Whiteman's Gap. They were greeted by a spectacular valley with wonderful lakes, hemmed in on both sides with peaks that were nothing but awe-inspiring.

Sinclair and his group, led by his guide Mackipictoon, crossed the Great Divide via White Man Pass to the Cross River on the western side of the Rockies. From here they followed the Kootenay River, finally entering the narrow defile today known as Sinclair Canyon and emerging a little north of Lake Windermere on the Columbia River. They reached Fort Vancouver in the fall of that year.

In 1845, two other parties were to use the same route as Sinclair, but for entirely different reasons. Travelling west along the Bow Valley and then up the Spray Valley to Oregon were Lieutenants H.J. Warre and M. Vavasour. They were on a secret military mission for the British War Office, under the instructions of the Governor General of Canada, to assess the "capabilities" of the Oregon Territory "in

Mt. Lougheed

Mt. Sparrowhawk

a military point of view". In essence, they were British spies. After an arduous, injury-plagued journey during which many horses were lost, they concluded that the steep mountain passes, swamps, and impenetrable forests would not be feasible for the deployment of troops. That same year, Father de Smet was guided over the same route in the opposite direction, coming from Lake Pend Oreille in Idaho, and met Warre and Vavasour. De Smet was on a mission to spread peace and Christianity to the warring Blackfoot nation.

The Legend of the Dead Grizzly

In 1914, the Spray Lakes were the scene of one of the most bizarre grizzly maulings in the annals of bear attacks. Apparently Oscar Lovgren, a young Swede working at the Spray Lake lumber camp, reported that he had killed a troublesome bear by firing five bullets into the bruin. After lunch, he and two companions returned to the scene of the killing in order to skin the bear and obtain the meat, only to find that the bear had disappeared.

Following a trail of blood, they found the wounded animal. With a blood-curdling roar, the wounded grizzly rose to her feet and made straight for Lovgren, who was carrying the rifle. With one swipe, the

Mounts Lougheed and Sparrowhawk look entirely different when viewed from the western shores of Spray Lakes Reservoir, 2.8 km south of Three Sisters Dam.

grizzly tore off the man's face and crushed his skull. The other two men escaped and made their way back to camp to report this incident. Warden Howard Sibbald arrived to investigate the scene and found the dead grizzly no more than 200 yards from where the animal had killed the young Swede. Sibbald investigated the carcass of the bear and found that it did indeed contain five bullet holes! A coroner's jury returned a verdict of accidental death.

James Sinclair (c. 1806–1856)

James Sinclair

James Sinclair must be recognized as one of the great historical figures associated with discovery and exploration in the Kananaskis region. As the first person of European heritage to explore the Spray Lakes region and the first to cross what is now North Kananaskis Pass, this recognition is long overdue.

The exact date of James Sinclair's birth is uncertain, but it was sometime around 1806. His father, William, had come from the Orkney Islands to work for the Hudson's Bay Company. At the time of James' birth, he held a post at Oxford House on the Hayes River, and a few years later would be appointed a Chief Factor. James's mother Nahovway (also the mother of William's ten other children) was half Cree.

James Sinclair was proud of his Métis ancestry, or what was then called 'half-breed' or 'mixed blood' ancestry. He sought liberty and free trade for the Red River Métis for most of his life. Originally applied to children of French and Native ancestry, the term Métis later became associated with all persons of mixed European and Native blood. The Métis became an integral part of the fur trade and by Sinclair's time many had risen to positions of importance.

James Sinclair was intelligent, articulate, and wise in the ways of the western frontier. He was fortunate in that his father had made provision for his formal education at Edinburgh University in Scotland, from which he graduated. He was more than a casual acquaintance of many influential fur magnates of the day, including General Henry Ashley and John Jacob Astor, and even had occasion to become befriended by the great Ulysses S. Grant himself.

Sinclair was not a great fan of Sir George Simpson. Against the policies of the Hudson's Bay Company, Sinclair was one of only a handful of men who promoted free trade, which brought him into disfavour with Simpson. In addition, the 'Little Governor' had had an unhappy affair with James' sister Betsy, which resulted in the birth of an illegitimate daughter on February 10, 1822. Sinclair was nevertheless sophisticated enough to forego any resentment he might harbour, due to Simpson's limitless power as Governor of the Hudson's Bay Company. In an effort to rid the Company of this 'free-trader' and to fortify British claim to the disputed Oregon Territory, Simpson in 1854 hired Sinclair to guide a group of

British subjects from the Red River settlement across the Rockies to settle at Walla Walla, Oregon.

It is ironic that a man who spent most of his life advocating the rights of Indians died at their hands. True to his courageous nature, James Sinclair died in a hail of bullets trying to save the life of a wife of a workman during an uprising on the Columbia River in Oregon on March 26, 1856.

First Trip Across the Rockies

On June 3, 1841, Sinclair, along with a group of Métis emigrants, set forth from Fort Garry on the Red River across the prairies, intent on crossing the Rockies in order to settle in the then-disputed Oregon Territory. Reaching Fort Edmonton in August, Sinclair hired the great Chief of the Wetaskiwin Crees, Mackipictoon (see his story on page 131) to guide the party across the mountains.

Mackipictoon assured Sinclair that he knew of a new route through the mountains that no white man had ever travelled—just what Sinclair wanted. Sir George Simpson had left instructions at Fort Edmonton for Sinclair's party to cross the mountains via Jasper House and then the Athabasca Pass to Oregon. Disregarding Simpson's explicit instructions, Sinclair prepared to guide his party across the Rockies by a new route he intended to discover himself.

Mackipictoon guided the party from Fort Edmonton through Devil's Gap near the mountain known as Devil's Head at the entrance to the Rockies. They reached the long narrow lake known to the Assiniboine Indians as *Minnee-wah-kah*, or the

Ancient pictographs on the rock walls leading through Whiteman's Gap above Canmore

Lake Where the Spirits Dwell. The Cree had a more foreboding name for the lake, *Much-Manitou-sa-gi-agun,* which means The Devil's Lake. After a short stay at the lake, their guide took them to the valley of the Bow River, probably along Carrot Creek. They entered the Bow River Valley near present-day Canmore, where they were impressed with the triple summits of what we know today as the Three Sisters.

From here Mackipictoon took them through Whiteman's Gap, above present-day Canmore between Mt. Rundle and Ha Ling Peak. If you think the secondary road up this defile is rough and a bit intimidating today, imagine how it must have felt to these explorers as they led their horses up this steep, rocky incline over 150 years ago, not knowing what they would encounter on the other side! Mackipictoon must have learned of this route by word of mouth passed down for generations by aboriginal hunters. We know the route had been used for centuries because travellers left evidence in the form of pictographs on the cliff faces. If you explore the upper canyon past the beautiful Grassi Lakes, you can view these ancient drawings. Remember not to touch them, though, as the oil from your hands will hasten their decay.

A splendid view of the waterfalls in Whiteman's Gap, still frozen in late May

129

Spray Lakes Reservoir from the summit of Mount Sparrowhawk

Once through the gap, the group entered a country of majestic peaks and lakes. Sinclair and his party were the first people, after the Natives, known to have gazed upon the Spray Lakes.

The Stoney gave the lakes the name *Horgatabi Mne* ('The Lake where fish were netted and trapped'). It was also called *Mne thto* ('Long narrow lake'). For centuries, before the coming of the white men, fish were apparently trapped in nets constructed of braided sinew set below the outlet of the river.

Travel was exhilarating in this high country as Sinclair's group passed peaks we now know as Buller, Nestor, Engadine and Fortune. Crossing the Great Divide at a pass known today as White Man Pass, they were finally able to gaze upon waters that flowed toward the Pacific Ocean. The group eventually reached its destination in the autumn of 1841.

Discovery of Kananaskis Pass

Sinclair came through the Kananaskis again in 1854 with a party consisting of 15 families, a band of about 100 Cree, and 250 head of oxen and horses, to lead the first confirmed expedition into the Kananaskis Valley.

They were led along the ancient Forks Trail or the *Ozade Chagu*. This ancient pack trail had been used for centuries to get to various hunting grounds, to the Kananaskis Lakes for fishing, and to suitable berry-picking locations. The trail was also used as the route across the Great Divide, where trading between the tribes occurred. Mackipictoon had assured Sinclair that a new route up the Strong Current River (the Kananaskis) over an unknown pass was a preferred route to Oregon Territory.

Travel up the valley was difficult. The birth of a baby who died a few days later at Bow Camp, at the confluence of the Bow and Kananaskis rivers, delayed the party for three weeks and was an omen of the hardships to come. They encountered deadfall from strong winds and the remains of forest fires.

After the Cree had abandoned the party at Morley, Sinclair continued to the Kananaskis Lakes, where Mackipictoon became hopelessly lost. Sinclair then took over and guided the party by compass. They apparently crossed what is now Turbine Canyon by a crude log bridge and thence over North Kananaskis Pass through three feet of snow in October 1854. The journey across the pass from Old Bow Fort had taken the party thirty days. In 1841 it had only taken ten days for Sinclair's party to cross White Man Pass.

Although there is some confusion as to which pass they actually crossed—the North or the South Kananaskis Pass—the South pass appears to be out of the question owing to a steep headwall that could not have been crossed by the cattle and horses.

Whatever the route, James Sinclair was the first person of European descent known to have navigated Kananaskis Valley and crossed North Kananaskis Pass, even though Captain John Palliser is given credit for the discovery of this famous pass.

Mackipictoon

Mackipictoon is another of the forgotten legends of Kananaskis lore. He has been relegated to the back pages of history, and yet this Cree Indian guide played a prominent role in the discovery of two major passes across the Great Divide.

Mackipictoon's place in history is complicated by the fact that he was apparently referred to by various names during his life. His name in Cree means 'Broken Arm' or 'Deformed Arm', and has many translations in Cree, Blackfoot, French and English. He is referred to as Mackipictoon, Maski-pitoon, Maskipiton, Maskepetoon or Maskapetoon, depending on the author. There is also confusion over the existence of two separate men with the same name. Palliser's Indian guide, a Cree named Nichiwa, may actually have been Mackipictoon.

Mackipictoon was a Chief of the Wetaskiwin Cree. It is unclear whether his broken arm was a childhood deformity or the result of an accident during battle. His alertness and sharp eyesight also led to his other name, 'He who has eyes behind him'. Various sources have described Mackipictoon as "imposing" and "kingly", and that he was a "magnificent looking man physically and was keen and intelligent".

Mackipictoon had a reputation among his Cree brethren of being a courageous, savage, and sometimes cruel brave who displayed commanding skill in gathering scalps and stealing horses. Mackipictoon had passed all of the Cree endurance and bravery

Mackipictoon, the great Cree Chief, from a reproduction of a painting made by George Catlin in 1832

practices, including fasting and physical mortification, and in due time became a chief of whom his tribesmen were proud. He was also a well-travelled warrior and diplomat who received a special audience with U.S. President Andrew Jackson when he visited the American capital. His diplomacy was evident at the Fort Laramie Treaty Council in 1851 and at the Judith River Treaty in 1855.

During a chance meeting with James Sinclair at Fort Edmonton in 1841, Mackipictoon informed him of negotiable passes through the Rocky Mountains that were untrodden by any white man. Only then do we begin to learn more of this unusual Cree Indian.

The Apostle of Peace

Unfortunately, Mackipictoon had an uncontrollable temper. It was even said that he had once scalped his wife for her suspected infidelity, and that she had miraculously survived the ordeal.

His temperament improved greatly after he was converted to Christianity by the Reverend R.T. Rundle, less than one year before being hired by Sinclair to guide his party across the Rockies. His conversion to Christianity convinced him that killing and violence were wrong, and he devoted his life to the way of peace. Even the murder of his father could not dissuade Mackipictoon from this peaceful mission. He quickly became known as an 'Apostle of Peace'. Grant MacEwan, in his book *Fifty Mighty Men*, called -

Mackipictoon "The Gandhi of the Prairies".

This devotion to peace would eventually prove to be his undoing. Around 1869, Mackipictoon was attempting to arrange another truce between the Cree and Blackfoot tribes when a young Blackfoot brave sud-denly mortally wounded the 'Apostle of Peace'. His death was not in vain, however, as the settlers around Fort Edmonton were grateful for the security his peace initiatives had provided them. This was the nature of the man who led Sinclair through the Rocky Mountains in 1841 and again in 1854.

Peaks of the Spray Valley

Mt. Nestor

Mount Nestor from the Spray Lakes day use area on the Smith-Dorrien/ Spray Trail

Mount Nestor 2975 m

Mount Nestor is the southern-most peak of the Goat Range, which forms the boundary between Kananaskis Country and Banff National Park. It was named after HMS *Nestor*, a member of the Thirteenth Destroyer Flotilla under the command of The Honorable Edward Bingham at the Battle of Jutland.

M. Toft and J. Martin recorded the first ascent of Mt. Nestor in 1975, via the easy east ridge.

Now Where Shall We Go?

At the Battle of Jutland, HMS *Nestor* and her sister ships HMS *Nomad* and HMS *Nicator* made one of the most courageous destroyer attacks in British naval history as they waded into German Scouting Group I. Out-numbered and outgunned, they pressed their attack on the German cruisers, and all were badly hit by German fire. Severely damaged, *Nestor* swung wildly, barely missing *Nicator*, but was then inadvertently rammed by *Nomad*. For a time her life seemed charmed, but at last she shook and trembled under the impact of direct hits. Officers and crewmen made their last preparations, as the *Nestor* had to finish in the style of British tradition.

Splinters of flying steel cut down the men, and water rushed through holes in her sides as *Nestor* began to list to starboard. Remaining on deck, Commander Bingham asked his young lieutenant, Bethell, "Now where shall we go?" "To Heaven, I trust, Sir," replied Bethell. Bethell then ran to the aid of a mortally wounded man but a shell burst over his head and the young lieutenant disappeared, making his exit from life's stage.

The *Nestor's* bow rose high out of the water and she was given three cheers by her surviving crew. Her stern then pointed almost vertically into the sky and she was given a last salute of "God save the King" by the men in the lifeboats. The *Nestor* indeed finished in style.

A German destroyer rescued the eighty surviving crewmen, including Commander Bingham. Bingham spent the next two and a half years in a German prisoner of war camp. He described the *Nestor's* final moments in a letter to his wife. "There we lay for a few awful moments, the enemy masses looming up nearer and nearer and not a friend in sight. It was a relief when the shells arrived. I knew it was only a matter of a few minutes so I gave the order, 'Abandon ship; every man for himself.' We took to the boats: the *Nestor* sank a few seconds later. We gave three cheers as she went down, then sang 'Tipperary' and 'The King'."

Old Goat Mtn.

Old Goat Mountain 3125 m

Old Goat Mountain is an unofficial name, and rumour has it that it refers to a certain individual in the Banff area. Captain Palliser named the entire range from the translation of the Stoney name, *Kiska tha Iyarhe*. The first recorded ascent of Old Goat occurred in 1974, when W. Davis, F. Campbell, and P. Vermeulen reached the summit in 4 1/2 hours, only to find a cairn with no record of a previous ascent.

The Goat Range with its dominant peak, Old Goat Mountain, viewed from the Mount Sparrowhawk day use area on the Smith-Dorrien/Spray Trail

Spies in the Kananaskis

In his 1845 inaugural address, U.S. President James K. Polk declared that the United States should lay claim to all of Oregon and the entire region from the Rockies to the Pacific from Mexico to Russian America (Alaska). Both British Prime Minister Sir Robert Peel and his foreign minister, the Earl of Aberdeen, had turned down Hudson's Bay Company governor George Simpson's request to send four warships into the region. Instead, the Prime Minister agreed to send a pair of undercover agents west, "To gain a general knowledge of the capabilities of the Oregon Territory in a military point of view, in order that we may be enabled to act immediately

Pass in the Rocky Mountains, by Henry Warre, July 24, 1845

and with effect in defense of our rights in that quarter, should those rights be infringed by any hostile aggression or encroachment on the part of the United States."

Lieutenant Henry J. Warre, aide to the Governor General of Canada, and Lieutenant Mervin Vavasour of the Royal Engineers were chosen for this mission. They were to disguise themselves as gentlemen visiting the west "for the pleasure of field sports and scientific pursuit." Warre was also an accomplished artist (see above and page 21) and prepared some fine sketches and watercolors for a book entitled *Sketch of a Journey Across the Continent of North America from Canada to the Oregon Territory and the Pacific Ocean*. Warre was impressed with the scenery but became well aware of the difficulties of reaching and crossing the Great Divide. On approaching the Spray Valley, he wrote, "Am traversing a narrow valley and crossing into a fine open plain,

with fine stream running through the center. Continuing on our route and passing two or three small but very beautifully situated lakes round which we were obliged to pass through swamps & the thickest kind of thick wood, we camped on another small prairie completely imbedded in the mountains."

Warre and Vavasour basically followed the same route as that taken by James Sinclair in 1841 over White Man Pass, and they reached Fort Vancouver on August 12, 1845. In the process, over half of their sixty horses lost their lives, convincing the pair that the idea of supplying a military force by a route across the Great Divide was quite impractical.

Their spying mission lasted for six months. By the time they returned to Montreal with their final report, British Prime Minister Robert Peel had already decided to yield the area between the Columbia River and the 49th parallel to the Americans.

Father De Smet (1801-1873)

Ode to the Rocky Mountains

*All hail! Majestic Rock –
the home
Where many a wanderer yet
shall come,
Where God Himself from His
own heart,
Shall health and peace and joy
impart.*

Pierre-Jean de Smet

The First Black Robe Across the Great Divide

Pierre-Jean de Smet, of Flemish descent, arrived in America in 1821 as a twenty-year-old Jesuit novitiate, contrary to his father's wishes. He spent most of his time at the Jesuit seminary in Missouri, where he became a priest in 1827. At the age of thirty-eight he answered the call of the wilderness to visit the Salish Indians of western North America. Father de Smet was the first 'Black Robe' to visit and cross the Great Divide north of the 49th parallel.

Guided by some young Kootenay Indians, Father de Smet left Lake Pend Oreille at Clark's Fork, Idaho and crossed the Great Divide at White Man Pass in 1845. He was on a mission to convert the Plains Blackfoot to Christianity. His group then followed the valley containing the Spray Lakes for three days before emerging at the Bow River near present-day Canmore. This de Smet accomplished although greatly overweight — a fact he was well aware of, even to the point of joking to others about his condition. For his return trip over the Athabasca Pass, de Smet went on a drastic diet, losing over 30 pounds. By coincidence, this was the same year that Warre and Vavasour, two young British officers, entered the valley for entirely different reasons (see previous section).

De Smet's route is difficult to follow in his journals, but George Dawson of the Geological Survey of Canada was certain that the route crossed the same pass as that crossed by James Sinclair in 1841. De Smet mentions erecting a "Cross of Peace" on the pass, and Natives had told Dawson of seeing remnants of this cross on the summit of White Man Pass. In fact, the pass itself may have been named by the Natives in honour of the Black Robe, rather than after the emigrants who accompanied James Sinclair across the pass in 1841.

After 1847, and for the remainder of his life, Father de Smet was an advocate of peace. He was a trusted emissary at many treaty negotiations and was an active participant at the 1851 Fort Laramie Treaty. He was even instrumental in securing the treaty in the 1868 Fort Laramie negotiations with Sittting Bull, thereby diffusing the threat of war, even though the government broke its promises less than a decade later.

Father Pierre-Jean de Smet

The Elbow River Region

The Elbow River Valley

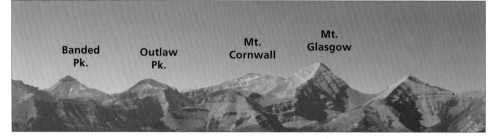

Banded Pk.   Outlaw Pk.   Mt. Cornwall   Mt. Glasgow

The Elbow Group

James Hector wrote these words in his journal when he passed this way in the summer of 1858:

After a few miles we reached Swiftwater Creek...and followed up the valley of the creek in full sight of the mountains, which were completely covered with snow although it was only mid-August. The country here is exceedingly beautiful.

The Elbow River arises in the Highwood Pass region from the glacier beneath the slopes of Mt. Rae. Numerous alpine streams feed the river before it enters the foothills. It ends on the prairie, where it joins the Bow River at Calgary. Much of the area through which the Elbow River flows is rugged backcountry, with the hamlet of Bragg Creek being the only major settlement in the area. Although both Sibbald and Jumpingpound Creeks originate north of the Elbow River and flow into the Bow River near Cochrane, they are included in this drainage basin because their history is closely intertwined with that of the Elbow River region. The entire region is steeped in rich human history dating back thousands of years. When you enter the Elbow River region of

Kananaskis Country via either Elbow Falls Trail (Hwy. 66), or Sibbald Creek Trail (Hwy. 68), you will be travelling over routes that archeological evidence suggests were used by humans more than ten thousand years ago.

The Elbow River: Origins

The Elbow Falls Trail basically follows the ancient Stoney trail called *Mnotha Wapta Chagu*. This was the Crackling River Trail the Stoney used as a pack trail to and from various locations in the mountains for hunting, fishing, trapping and berry-picking.

The Stoney knew the Elbow River as *Mnotha wapta*, meaning 'Swift Water' or 'Crackling Water' Creek. It was obviously named for the sound it emits as it rushes over the small rapids. The headwaters of the river, or *Mnotha Wapta Ipta Imne*, which originate at diminutive Rae Glacier beneath the slopes of Mt. Rae and Elbow Lake, are the ultimate source of the drinking water for most of the population of Calgary.

Two branches of the Elbow River, the Big and Little Elbow, flow through beautiful and isolated rugged mountain backcountry before converging near the present-day Elbow River

Recreation Area. Headwaters of the Little Elbow River are found in the Opal Range. The river then enters the foothills and joins with the Bow River in Calgary. The Little Elbow River was known to the Stoney as the creek where a cougar was shot and killed, or *Ihmotaga Mostagabi Waptan.*

Stories abound regarding the origin of the name 'Elbow'. One suggests that the name *Ispa Wapta* originated when an Indian brave named Walking Beaver fell off his horse and broke his arm during a hunting excursion, but there is no evidence to substantiate this. A more likely origin of the name is its reference to the bend in the river, which resembles the elbow of an arm. Elbow Falls or 'Small Waterfalls' were called *Mini Oyade.*

In 1911 the city of Calgary proposed the construction of a hydroelectric dam on the Elbow River near Canyon Creek. How fortunate it is that engineering studies indicated an inadequate reservoir storage capacity, as such a dam would have destroyed Elbow Falls and much of the valley to the west in the foothills. The only direct evidence of human interference with the flow of the Elbow River has been the construction of Allen Bill Pond, completed in 1983, and Forgetmenot Pond in the Little Elbow Recreation Area. Both were constructed from floodplain deposits of the Elbow.

Early Exploration

Very few specific references to the Elbow River survive from the days of early explorers, but James Gaddy did spend three winters with the Peigan Indians in the late 1700s, and it is hard to believe he did not enter the region. It is known that David Thompson crossed the Elbow about eight kilometres downstream of present-day Bragg Creek on his way to winter with the Peigan Indians in 1787-88, but he did not explore the upper reaches of the valley. Only one

Rae Glacier, the source of the Elbow River

trading post operated in the area— the Hudson's Bay Company's Peigan Post in the Bow Valley, and it closed in 1835 after two futile years.

As mentioned, James Hector, coleader of the Palliser Expedition, reached the 'Swiftwater Creek' and followed it up the valley in the summer of 1858. His party even tried its hand at fishing using some common twine, and caught 36 trout in less than an hour and a half.

The Whisky Forts

In 1870, a few years after the formation of the Dominion of Canada in 1867, the Hudson's Bay Company turned over ownership and administration of Rupert's Land to the fledgling nation. Trouble arose when the government failed to establish firm authority over these vast western territories. One of the first groups to take advantage of this were American 'free traders', who realized that quick wealth was available in the whisky trade. The illegality of this trade and the misery it would bring to the Native people mattered little to these men. They established the first of the whisky posts near Fort Macleod. It became known as the infamous Fort Whoop-Up.

Two whisky forts grew up in the Elbow River region. The first was built in 1871 by Fred Kanouse, a deputy

Elbow Falls are a favourite tourist attraction

sheriff from Montana. Relations between the Indians and the traders became violent, resulting in the killing of a Blood Indian named White Eagle. In order to avenge this death, the Bloods set siege to the fort in a battle that lasted three days. Later, a trader known as 'Liver Eating Johnston' and a friend arrived to drive off the Bloods and relieve the trapped men. Kanouse eventually returned to Montana to resume duties as a deputy sheriff, but not before returning in 1872 for another season of illicit trade.

The following year Dick Berry erected another post on the Elbow River, approximately twenty kilometres upstream from Kanouse, probably near present-day Bragg Creek. Violence led to Berry's death at the hands of a Blood Indian named Old Woman's Child, whom he had previously cheated out of precious furs.

It has been estimated that in just over two years in southern Alberta, 12,000 gallons of liquor were traded to the Indians in exchange for $150,000 worth of furs—a considerable sum in those days.

The North West Mounted Police

In 1872 the Canadian government responded to the whisky trading by sending Colonel P. Robertson-Ross, the commanding officer and adjutant-general of the Canadian Militia, to investigate. His report documented the demoralization, bloodshed, and injury the Natives were suffering from the illicit traffic. "The demoralization of the Indians and injury to the country from this illicit traffic is very great," he wrote.

His report led to the creation of the North West Mounted Police by Sir John A. Macdonald during the parliamentary session of 1873. It was a successful move. By the end of 1874 most of the whisky traders had abandoned their posts and fled southward across the border. The return of law and order as well as the signing of Treaty

No. 7 opened the way for settlers to move into the area.

Early Settlement

The Dominion Lands Act passed by Parliament in 1872 provided 160 acres of land for a $10 fee to anyone who could establish a farm or ranch on the land within a three-year period. What a steal! Early ranchers in the area included Sam Livingstone (for whom the Livingstone Range is named), Senator M.H. Cochrane (for whom the town of Cochrane was named),

A.W. Bragg (for whom the creek and hamlet were named), and John and T.K. Fullerton (whose mountain bears their name).

In the 1890s, George Ings discovered a coal seam in the region, but had little success in selling it. Much later, in 1914, the first attempt to extract petroleum occurred in the area near present day Bragg Creek Provincial Park, at the Mowbray-Berkley well. The marginal output of the well led to its being shut down several years later.

The Mountains Closest To Calgary

Moose Mountain
2473 m

Moose Mountain is the mountain closest to Calgary. The name is descriptive and there is no record of its first ascent. Topped by a fire lookout since 1929, it occupies a strategic position as it overlooks a wide range of the Elbow River Region.

The mountain has had an interesting history. A.W. Bragg homesteaded on its lower slopes in 1886, and George Ings discovered coal in the area in the 1890s. More recently, natural gas was discovered, and Shell opened the Moose Mountain Compressor Station in 1985. Five wells feed the station with the gas, which travels by pipeline and is processed at the Quirk Creek gas plant 28 km to the south.

The Stoney Indians referred to this peak as *Iyarhe Wida,* which means

either 'The Island Mountain' or 'The Mountain by Itself.' This is quite remarkable, as geologists now know that the mountain is an 'inlier'—a geologic structure in which a mass of older Paleozoic rock is surrounded by much younger rock of Mesozoic origin. Moose Mountain was formed by several thrust faults occurring in close proximity to each other, resulting in the stacking of older rock on top of younger rock.

The ice caves are perhaps the best known feature of Moose Mountain. They were discovered by Stan Fullerton in 1905. These caves were formed

Moose Mtn.

Moose Mountain from the summit of Powderface Ridge

Entrance to the Moose Mountain Ice Caves

by the seepage of groundwater, over aeons, through the limestone rock. Experienced spelunkers have mapped over 500 metres of subterranean passageways in four different caverns of the extensive cave system, which penetrates deep within the mountain.

Powderface Ridge

Prairie Mtn.

Prairie Mountain and Powderface Ridge

The sulphurous odor associated with the groundwater in the region, and in particular with Canyon Creek, is due to springs flowing through bedrock containing the sour and very poisonous hydrogen sulphide gas.

Prairie Mountain 2205 m

Diminutive Prairie Mountain lies just south of Moose Mountain, separated from it by Canyon Creek. Its name refers to the splendid views of the prairies one gets looking east from the summit. The Stoneys called Prairie Mountain *Iyarhe wida tagichuwaga*, which means 'The Younger Brother of Island Mountain', referring of course to Moose Mountain.

Prairie Mountain has become the early season conditioner for hikers. Due to the ever-present chinook winds, the ridge leading to its summit remains snow-free for much of the year, and for this reason parties can be found hiking to the top in any season. Good views of both Prairie and Moose Mountains can be had from the Elbow Falls Trail just prior to Allen Bill Pond, where both peaks lie almost directly in front of you.

Ridges of the Elbow Valley

Forgetmenot Ridge

Powderface Ridge
2210 m

When you travel west on Elbow River Trail and come to the entrance to Beaver Flats campground, the unnamed piece of rubble to your left guarding the entrance to the valley is *Iyahre Ipan,* the Stoney name for 'Mountain Corner'. You then begin the steep climb to the summit of Rainy Pass, where the entire length of Powderface Ridge comes into view.

Powderface Ridge was named for Tom Powderface and his family, Stoney Indians who lived in the area around 1949. They would have known it by its Stoney name, *Thide thaba Baha,* which means 'Mule deer buck

hill'. The creek also bears his name. The outcroppings on the summit contain an abundance of brachiopod fossils.

Forgetmenot Ridge
and Mountain 2335 m

Both the mountain and the 8-km-long ridge were named for the brilliant blue-flowered Alpine Forget-Me-Not *(Myosotis alpestris).* This alpine beauty is the favourite of almost every hiker. It is the official state flower of Alaska.

Forgetmenot Mountain was the site of a fire lookout until 1975. At that time it was removed, and all that remains today is the concrete foundation. The broad, grassy ridge, accessible to the strong hiker

Alpine Forget-Me-Not

The north and south summits of Forgetmenot Ridge

Nihahi Ridge

Nihahi Ridge from the Elbow River Recreation Area, is a great spot to observe alpine flowers, and at a small outcropping

below the north summit, one can also observe brachiopod fossils. This ridge looks spectacular from the summit of Rainy Pass

Nihahi Ridge 2530 m

Nihahi is the Stoney term for a rocky or steep cliff mountain, which aptly describes this 7-km-long ridge. Nihahi Ridge is best viewed from higher elevations, but good sites occur along Ford Creek Road (an extension of Hwy. 66) or from Forgetmenot Pond day use area along the Elbow River.

The Battle of Coronel: Prelude To the Falklands

Good Hope **prior to being sunk at Coronel, Chile**

In 1914, following some operations in the Pacific, the German East Asiatic Squadron of five cruisers, under the command of Vice Admiral Maximilian von Spee, decided to return to Germany via Cape Horn. British Rear Admiral Sir Christopher Cradock became aware of the German presence and sailed a small force into Chilean waters to confront this overwhelming force. His inferior fleet consisted of three armoured cruisers, his flagship HMS *Good Hope*, as well as HMS *Glasgow* and HMS *Monmouth*, an armed merchant cruiser (HMS *Otranto*), and an old, slow battleship, the HMS *Canopus*, which trailed this main fleet by some three hundred miles. In addition, Cradock's crew consisted mostly of reservists, who had carried out only one practice shoot!

Why did Cradock press his luck against these overwhelming odds? No one will ever know, as the answer lies at the bottom of the South Pacific. On November 1, 1914, the outgunned British squadron met von Spee at Coronel, located approximately 322 km south of Valparaiso off the coast of Chile, and the Royal Navy suffered its most humiliating defeat in a hundred years. In short order the *Monmouth* and *Good Hope* were each hit over thirty times, and explosions were going on everywhere. Finally, less than fifty minutes after the start of the battle, a terrible explosion ripped the *Good Hope* apart with flames reaching a height of over 200 feet, after which she disappeared. *Monmouth*, belching flames from her deck and flooding from gaping holes blasted into her hull, met a similar fate. In keeping with British naval tradition, neither ship surrendered. Sixteen hundred Royal Navy crewmen, including their bold commander Christopher Cradock, were lost in the battle.

The First Canadian Naval Casualties of World War I

It is not commonly known that the first casualties of World War I suffered by the Royal Canadian Navy occurred at Coronel. The Canadian seamen killed at the Battle of Coronel were Midshipman William Archibald Palmer of Ottawa, and three midshipmen from Nova Scotia: John V. W. Hatheway of Granville, Malcolm Cann of Yarmouth, and Arthur Wiltshire Silver of Halifax. The four young midshipmen were doing their 'big ship time' aboard the *Good Hope* when they perished with the rest of their shipmates. Rear Admiral Cradock had specifically requested Midshipmen Silver and Palmer, while Cann and Hatheway were drawn by lot.

Sir Christopher Cradock (1862–1914)

Cradock joined the Royal Navy in 1875. Just before World War I he was appointed commander of the North America and West Indies station, where his principal wartime responsibility was the protection of the main British trade routes in the region. He was ordered to search for Vice Admiral von Spee's East Asiatic Squadron, and for some reason decided to engage the vastly superior German fleet off Coronel. Cradock must receive total blame for recklessly engaging the German fleet. Why did he attack a numerically superior enemy force when it became evident that he was outgunned, outnumbered, and outranged? His only reward was a watery grave and an immortal place in the history of Royal Navy disasters.

When news of the disaster reached England, Rear Admiral Sir Robert Arbuthnot paid Cradock a final tribute when he said, "Poor Kit Cradock. He always hoped he would be killed in battle or break his neck in the hunting field." Sir Christopher got his wish at Coronel.

Sir Christopher Cradock

Admiral Maximilian von Spee (1861–1914)

Vice Admiral von Spee, Commander of the German East Asiatic Squadron, made a critical error after defeating the British squadron off Coronel. Instead of making directly for Germany, where his great victory would have resulted in his appointment to Commander of the German High Seas Fleet, Von Spee made the mistake of attacking the British squadron at the Falkland Islands. Just as we will never know Cradock's motives at Coronel, there is no way of knowing why von Spee chose to attack the Falklands. Britain finally avenged the Coronel disaster when von Spee, two thousand of his men, and all his battle cruisers were lost in the Battle of the Falklands.

Vice Admiral Maximilian von Spee

The Battle of the Falklands

After suffering the loss of two battle cruisers and close to 1,600 seamen at Coronel, the Royal Navy was bent on revenge. On November 11, 1914, the battle cruisers HMS *Invincible* and HMS *Inflexible* under Admiral Doveton Sturdee were dispatched to the Falkland Islands. They arrived at Port Stanley on December 11 to join the *Kent, Carnarvon, Cornwall, Glasgow, Bristol, Macedonia*, and *Canopus* to form an imposing squadron.

Elated with his victory at Coronel, Vice Admiral von Spee hoped to surprise the Royal Navy at Port Stanley, but was completely unaware of the huge flotilla moored at the port. Overwhelmed by the sight of the size of the British fleet, Von Spee split his fleet in two and ordered a quick retreat. Had he realized that most of the British battle cruisers were immobilized and being refuelled in Stanley Harbour, von Spee could have inflicted another devastating defeat on the Royal Navy. Instead, his retreat ensured a watery grave for the German East Asiatic Fleet.

Admiral Sturdee quickly dispatched his battle cruisers after the German warships, chasing and then destroying the German fleet in the First Battle of the Falklands. In quick order, the *Scharnhorst* and the *Gneisenau* were caught and engaged by the *Inflexible, Invincible,* and *Carnarvon*. The *Scharnhorst*, after receiving over fifty hits, with three funnels down, on fire, and listing badly, disappeared beneath the sea with all hands, including von Spee. Shortly thereafter the *Gneisenau* sank, and her surviving crew jumped into the icy waters of the South Atlantic, clinging to any object they could find. Most perished from hypothermia, but the *Inflexible* did manage to save 190 members of her crew.

Glasgow, Cornwall, and *Kent* were sent in pursuit of the *Leipzig, Nurnberg,* and *Dresden*. The *Leipzig* was sunk in a battle with *Cornwall* and *Glasgow,* while the *Kent* sank the *Nurnberg* after hitting her 38 times. The captain of the *Leipzig* refused to surrender, and sat on the bridge smoking his last cigarette as she sank.

Only the *Dresden* managed to escape, and she was hunted for months in the South Pacific by the *Kent* and the *Glasgow*. Captain John Luce, who had escaped in the *Glasgow* at Coronel, got his final revenge when he sank *Dresden* in the Bay of Juan Fernandez off the coast of Chile. The last of von Spee's squadron had been destroyed and the Battle of the Falklands ended where it had started, off Chile.

In recognition of his massive victory at the Falklands, Doveton Sturdee was given command of the Fourth Battle Cruiser Squadron of the Grand Fleet. Later, in 1917, he was promoted to full Admiral and ended his naval career as Commander-in-Chief at the Nore.

The Royal Navy, under the leadership of Admiral Doveton Sturdee, was bent on revenge for its defeat at Coronel.

Mountains of the Little Elbow Group

Mt. Glasgow

Then his small cluster of peaks lies between the rivers of the Big Elbow to the south and the Little Elbow to the north. Officially these mountains are part of the Fisher Range, and are a distinctive part of the skyline from as far away as Calgary.

Mount Glasgow 2950 m

Mount Glasgow was named after the battle cruiser HMS *Glasgow*, which, as mentioned, took part in the Battles of Coronel and the Falklands during World War I. She was commanded by Captain John Luce, who barely escaped disaster at Coronel, but extracted his final revenge off the coast of Chile in the final encounter of the Falklands battle.

There is no recorded first ascent of the peak.

HMS Glasgow at Coronel

At Coronel, the German fleet pounded the inferior British cruisers, but the *Glasgow* remained unscathed for half an hour. She then received her only serious hit when a shell burst a six-foot hole in her hull just below the waterline. She was hit five more times, but only four of her crew were wounded. Miraculously, she somehow escaped, while the *Good Hope* and the *Monmouth* were both sunk.

HMS Glasgow at the Falklands: "Do you surrender?"

Five weeks after the Battle of Coronel, the *Glasgow* was part of the squadron that destroyed von Spee's German Fleet at the First Battle of the

Mount Glasgow

Glasgow was commanded by Captain John Luce

Mt. Cornwall   Mt. Glasgow   Outlaw Pk.

The eastern slopes of Mount Cornwall are another well-known landmark visible from Calgary. They hold snow well into the month of June.

Falklands. Both the *Glasgow* and *Cornwall* pursued the *Leipzig* when, on Dec. 8, 1914, two hundred miles south of the Falklands, their concentrated salvos crippled the German battle cruiser.

By 7:00 P.M. that fateful day, the *Leipzig* was burning fiercely and in such shambles that Captain John Luce held his fire and repeatedly signaled the German ship: "Am anxious to save life. Do you surrender?" Strangely, Captain Haun of the *Leipzig* failed to haul down her colours, whereupon the *Glasgow* once again unleashed another broadside. Many of the *Leipzig's* crew took shelter behind the gunshields, but were mown down by shell explosions and shrapnel. Of her crew that was seen to leap overboard into the frigid waters, only eighteen were saved, and Captain Haun was not among them. He was last seen lighting a cigar, walking toward the crumbling remains of his bridge, and then disappearing in an eruption of flames and oily black smoke.

The Glasgow in the South Pacific: Sinking the Dresden

For three months, in the South Pacific, the *Glasgow*, along with the *Kent*, pursued the *Dresden*, the only German warship to survive the Falklands battle. Finally they caught up with her on March 14, 1915, off the coast of Chile in the Bay of Juan Fernandez.

Captain John Luce did not hesitate over the niceties of international law that protected battleships for twenty-four hours when in neutral waters. Since the *Dresden* had exceeded her stay in neutral waters, the *Glasgow* and the *Kent* joined in scoring many hits on the enemy warship. Within three minutes the *Dresden* had suffered enough damage for her captain to hoist a white flag. However, while negotiations for a truce were going on, Captain Ludecke opened her sea valves and put scuttling charges in place to sink his own beleaguered battleship. The sinking of the *Dresden* brought closure to the battle that had begun off the coast of Chile five months earlier. The British government subsequently apologized to Chile for breaching her neutrality!

Mount Cornwall
2956 m

Cornwall, not Cornwell

Contrary to popular belief, Mount Cornwall was not named in honour of heroic young master John Travers Cornwell, who sacrificed his life on HMS *Chester* at the Battle of Jutland. Rather, it was named in honour of HMS *Cornwall*, the battle cruiser that took part in the Battle of the Falklands in 1914, where she aided HMS *Glasgow* in the sinking of the *Leipzig*. During this battle the *Cornwall* received the most damage, being struck eighteen times by the fire from the *Leipzig*. Amazingly, she suffered no casualties and no worse damage than two flooded coalbunkers. Only seven officers and eleven men from the *Leipzig* were rescued, and Captain W.M. Ellerton later regretted that an officer as brave as Captain Haun of the *Leipzig* was not one of them. After the Falklands battle, the *Cornwall* was ordered back to the North Atlantic, where she took part in the Battle of Jutland.

The Story of John Travers Cornwell

Boy First Class John Travers Cornwell was the sight-setter on the forecastle gun of the *Chester*. He was all of 16 years old and in the middle of a most bloody battle. Mortally wounded early in the action, and with the rest of his gun's crew dead or dying around him, he nevertheless dutifully remained standing at a most exposed post waiting for orders that would never come. "He felt he might be needed, as indeed he might have been," Captain Lawson wrote to his mother, "so he stayed there, standing and waiting, under heavy fire, with

Banded Pk.

Banded Peak from the summit of Forgetmenot Ridge

just his own brave heart and God's help to support him." Gradually Cornwell weakened and succumbed to his wounds. He was posthumously awarded the Victory Cross for bravery.

Banded Peak 2934 m

Banded Peak is aptly named for the horizontal rock band just beneath the summit of the mountain. This dark band makes the mountain one of the easiest to identify, as it is visible all months of the year. There are many excellent sites on the Elbow Falls Trail (Hwy. 66) from which to view Banded Peak, while the entire Little Elbow Group of peaks is best viewed from one of the high ridges in the region.

In August 1974, A. Brawn, J. Gardner, G. Kinnear, and P. Spear recorded the first ascent of Banded Peak. Not content, they traversed an Unnamed 2850-m peak two and a half kilome-

Threepoint Mtn.

Threepoint Mountain

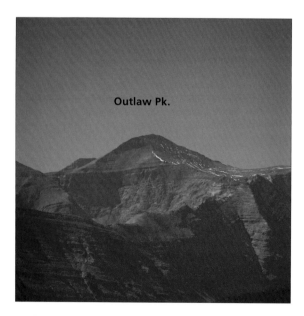

Outlaw Pk.

Outlaw Peak from the summit of Forgetmenot Ridge

Outlaw Peak 2970 m

For some reason, this major peak was ignored in 1922 when the other peaks in this cluster were being named after

tres southwest of Banded, ascended Outlaw Peak (2970 m), and continued with a traverse of both Mts. Cornwall and Glasgow. This was the first traverse of all the peaks in this grouping.

World War I battle cruisers. Don Forest, an Alpine Club of Canada official, named this peak 'Outlaw Peak' in 1974, mistakenly thinking that nearby Banded Peak was actually named 'Bandit Peak'. The party that made the first traverse of this group (see Banded Peak, above) also recorded the first ascent of Outlaw Peak.

Threepoint Mountain 2575 m

Five mountains — Bluerock, Rose, Burns, Threepoint and Cougar — form a small range just east of the main range between the Elbow and Sheep rivers. Only Threepoint and Cougar mountains are visible from the Little Elbow Recreation Area.

Cougar Mountain 2863 m

Cougar Mountain was named after the secretive and highly elusive cat that wanders these backcountry valleys and slopes. Only the fortunate few will ever have a chance to spot a cougar. While backpacking in the mid-1960s, I had my only encounter with this magnificent animal. Its unnerving crying went on well into the

Cougar Mtn.

evening, and it was only the next morning that we found evidence of its presence. Footprints in the freshly fallen snow about our campsite were as close as we ever came to sighting this retiring beast.

Cougar Mountain

Mountains North of the Little Elbow River

The peaks that lie to the north of the Little Elbow River technically belong to the Fisher Range. This range appears to have been named in 1859 by Palliser, in honour of Rev. George Fisher (1794–1873), a British astronomer and Arctic explorer who was an authority on the magnetic pole and the aurora borealis. The Fisher Range extends from Wasootch Ridge in the north to Mts. Romulus and Remus at the south. It lies between Evan-Thomas Creek to the west and Jumpingpound and Ford Creeks to the east.

Mt. Romulus   Mt. Remus

Mount Romulus (2832 m) and Mount Remus (2688 m)

Mounts Romulus and Remus

These two mountains are recognizable from almost anywhere due to their flat summits, which appear to

One can see Mounts Fullerton and Howard by ascending one of the ridges in the area. This is the view from the summit of Mount Fullerton.

have been sheared off by some gigantic force. Mt. Romulus can be identified by the large horizontal cornice of snow it often sports well into the summer months. Mt. Remus only appears to be the higher of the two mountains because Mt. Romulus lies about 1.5 km further west.

The first ascent of Mt. Remus was in 1965 by R. Allen and J. Martin up the southeast ridge. There is no information on the first ascent of Mt. Romulus, but in 1966 a party consisting of B. Fraser, E. Kinsey, R. Matthews, R. Peters and J. Tarrant climbed the peak and found a huge cairn built on the summit.

These twin peaks were given their mythological names in 1940. Romulus and his twin brother Remus were the sons of Mars, the Roman god of war, and Rhea Silvia, one of the vestal virgins. Romulus was the traditional founder and first king of Rome. Rhea Silvia was the daughter of Numitor, once the king of Alba Longa, who had been deposed by his younger brother Amulius. She had been made a priestess by her brother-in-law Amulius so that she would have no children to make claims against his throne. When Rhea Silvia became pregnant by Mars, Amulius was furious. When the twin boys were born, he had them placed into a basket and thrown into the Tiber River. The twins did not drown, but were rescued and nursed by a she-wolf on the slopes of the Palatine Hill. Later, they were discovered by a

shepherd, Faustulus, and reared by his wife Larentia until they grew into manhood. They then restored their grandfather, Numitor, to the throne.

The brothers then decided to build a city. After some quarreling about the spot, they finally choose the Palatine Hill. A wall was built around the hill to protect the city. Remus was displeased with the quality of the wall and scornfully leaped over it to demonstrate its inadequacy. Romulus was not amused by the actions of his twin brother, and killed him. Even today, Mt. Romulus looms dominantly over Mt. Remus, just as he did in ancient mythology.

Romulus became the first of seven kings to rule the city, which became the most powerful city in the world — Rome. He is said to have ruled from 753 to 716 B.C. As for his death, legend has it that he disappeared during a storm and was carried off by Mars.

Mount Fullerton
2728 m

Both Mount Fullerton and Mount Howard are difficult peaks to view, as they are almost completely hidden by Nihahi Ridge. There is no first ascent recorded for Mt. Fullerton. J. Martin made the first recorded ascent of Mt. Howard in 1978.

Which Fullerton?

There seems to be some confusion regarding the naming of this peak. Putnam and Boles, in *Place Names of the Canadian Alps* (1990), indicate that the mountain was named after Charles Percy Fullerton (1870–1938), Chairman of the Canadian Board of Railway Commissioners and later Chairman of the CNR.

Other evidence suggests that the mountain was named after a member of the Fullerton family who homesteaded in the area. Most probable is that the peak honours Ernest Redpath 'Jake' Fullerton (1882-1975), who

Jake Fullerton
with the sledge-
hammer at his
blacksmith
shop

helped his father, T.K., homestead in the area. Apparently Jake received his nickname from the name of one of his father's prized bulls. Jake, a boxer and blacksmith, set up his own ranch in the Bragg Creek area in 1914, and being an enterprising individual, also opened a store and a dancehall in the hamlet of Bragg Creek. He also set up the Wetmore & Fullerton Blacksmith shop next to the old Queen's Hotel on 8th Avenue in east Calgary around 1900.

His father, T.K. Fullerton, attempted to set up a lumbering operation on the Elbow River in the late 1880s, but twice met with disaster when early spring floods destroyed his booms and two winters' worth of labour.

Mount Howard 2777 m

Mount Howard was named in 1939 after Ted Howard, a British army officer who first came to the region in 1898. Returning again from his duties in the First World War, he became the Elbow District forest ranger for the next twenty years. As a ranger, Ted gained respect for his honesty and kindness, and above all, for the hard work he accomplished for the Alberta Forest Service.

As with Mt. Fullerton, you will have trouble viewing Mt. Howard from the Elbow Falls Trail as both Nihahi and Powderface Ridges block the view. If you wish to view this mountain you will have to hike up one of these two ridges, or, as in the earlier photo of Forgetmenot Ridge, scramble up that ridge.

Sibbald Flat: Ten Thousand Years of History

Sibbald Flat is the name given to a local channel that has been carved out of an outwash plain by glacial meltwaters, near the confluence of Jumpingpound and Sibbald creeks.

It is not entirely clear which member of the famous Sibbald family the Flat was named for. Perhaps it doesn't matter, as they were all prominent in the history of the Rocky Mountains.

A view of Sibbald Flat from the summit of Deer Ridge

Andrew (1833–1933) came to Morley in 1875, and as a missionary, taught school for Rev. McDougall. One of Andrew Sibbald's sons, Howard, was a guide and became the first chief game guardian of what was then Rocky Mountain Park (later Banff National Park). It appears likely, however, that the name honours Andrew's other son, Frank, who grew up at Morley and received the Stoney nickname *Tokun* ('The Fox'), in recognition of his superior tracking and hunting skills. Frank was also an efficient guide and packer for the CPR survey crew in 1882-83. He later began homesteading in the Jumpingpound Creek region in the 1890s near the creek and meadow that now probably bear his name.

A less endearing name for the area is *Siktothuthu Eyagubi Tida*, or 'Where they castrated a grey stallion clearing'. Apparently this is where the Stoney Indians used to graze a large herd of horses. A high-spirited grey stallion was causing all sorts of problems, even to the point of injuring many of the other horses. In order to calm him down, they castrated the stallion in the clearing that is now known as Sibbald Flat.

Andrew Sibbald, a Methodist Missionary, at age 25, circa 1858

The Fluted Point Tradition

During the summer of 1978, two archaeological sites, one in the Sibbald Flat campground and the other at the Pine Grove group camp, indicated the presence of prehistoric man in the area. The next year, during the reconstruction of Sibbald Creek Trail (Hwy. 68), an important archaeological site was unearthed just west of the present junction to Sibbald Lake. Construction of the road was delayed for over a year while Dr. Eugene M. Gryba of the University of Calgary's archaeology department led an extensive excavation of the site.

Over 17,000 artifacts, including projectile points, cutting and scraping tools, gravers for carving, drills, choppers, hammers, and other tools and fragments were unearthed. Most importantly, artifacts of the Fluted Point Tradition were discovered, which meant that the site had being used by hunters as long as ten thousand years ago. This has been confirmed by radioactive dating. This major find was the first discovery of fluted points in western Canada.

This was a site that was no doubt deliberately selected, as it offered a combination of the basic requisites for human survival—shelter and warmth, vantage over a large animal grazing range, and a general proximity to many natural resources. Protected from the cold north winds, its southeastern exposure received adequate sunshine, and its setting above the valley floor offered a commanding view of the grazing area. This site appears to have been used over the millennia by many cultures as each became supplanted by other, more advanced, cultures.

Cox Hill (2219 m) and Jumpingpound Mountain (2240 m)

These two minor peaks, not really mountains but high foothills, are part of the Moose Mountain panorama when viewed from the Trans-Canada Highway. Cox Hill was known to the Stoneys as *Zotha Odabi Baha* — a name that referred to the colony of hoary marmots that apparently once inhabited the rock outcroppings and talus slopes on the summit ridge. They have long since disappeared from the region.

Hoary marmots *(Marmota caligata)* occur almost exclusively in the alpine life zone, only occasionally being found in the montane zone, where talus slopes penetrate the forest. Their habit of whistling a loud, long note in the presence of danger gave them their other common name, 'the whistler'. The fur of these animals was much sought-after for the manufacture of garments by aboriginal peoples.

The Stoney Indians referred to Jumpingpound Mountain and creek as *Tokijarhpabi Wapta.* This name refers to the spot where the Blackfoot Indians, traditional enemies of the Stoney, camped. According to an old

legend, before peace existed between the two, this is where Stoney warriors clubbed a Blackfoot brave to death. In keeping with Blackfoot custom, the brave was laid to rest in his teepee at this site.

The summit of Jumpingpound Mountain

The hoary marmot *(Marmota caligata),* also known as 'the whistler'

Reference

Appleby, Edna. *Canmore: the story of an era.* Canmore: E.H. Appleby, 1975.

Beattie, Owen, and John Geiger. *Frozen in Time: Unlocking the Secrets of the Franklin Expedition.* Saskatoon: Western Producer Prairie Books, 1987.

Bennett, Geoffrey. *Coronel and the Falklands.* London: Batsford, 1962.

Bennett, Geoffrey. *The Battle of Jutland.* Newton Abbot [England]: David & Charles, 1972.

Boles, G.W., R. Kruszyna, and W.L. Putnam. *The Rocky Mountains of Canada South.* New York: The American Alpine Club; Banff: The Alpine Club of Canada, 1979.

Boyd, Larry. "Palliser's Lost Legacy." *Mountain Heritage Magazine,* 1999.

Brown, Annora. *Old Man's Garden.* Toronto: J.M. Dent & Sons, 1954.

Bunyan Ian et al. *No Ordinary Journey: John Rae, Arctic Explorer* 1813-1893. Montreal: McGill-Queen's University Press, 1993.

Campbell, Marjorie Wilkins. *The North West Company.* New York: Rinehart & Co., 1957.

Canadian Alpine Journal, 1916-1976.

Chalmers, William. *Dawson, Geologist, Scientist, Explorer.* Montreal: XYZ Publishing, 2000.

Chumak, Sebastian, Alfred Dixon, and Tomas T. Williams. *The Stonies of Alberta: An illustrated heritage of genesis, myths, legends, folklore, and wisdom of Yahey Wichastabi, the people-who-cook-with-hot stones / narrated by 12 Stoney Elders.* Calgary: Alberta Foundation, 1983.

Chiniki Research Team. *Ozade —Mnotha — Wapta —Makochi: Stoney Place Names.* Morley, Alberta: Chiniki Band, 1987.

Cole, Douglas, and Bradley J. Lockner, eds., *The Journals of George M. Dawson: British Columbia,* 1875-1878. Vancouver: University of British Columbia Press, 1989.

Costello, John & Terry Hughes. *Jutland, 1916.* London: Weidenfeld & Nicolson, 1976.

Dempsey, Hugh A. *Thompson's Journey to the Bow River.* Alberta Historical Review, Vol. 25, 1943.

de Smet, Father Pierre. *Oregon Missions and Travels over the Rocky Mountains in 1845-46.* New York: Edward Dunigan, 1847.

Erasmus, Peter, as told to Henry Thompson. *Buffalo Days and Nights.* Calgary: Fifth House, 1990.

Fraser, Esther. *The Canadian Rockies: Early Travels and Explorations.* Edmonton: M.G. Hurtig Ltd., 1969.

Frost, H.H. *The Battle of Jutland.* United States Naval Institute, 1936.

Gadd, B. *Handbook of the Canadian Rockies. 2nd ed.* Jasper, Alberta: Corax Press, 1995.

Galbraith, John S. *The Little Emperor: Governor Simpson of the Hudson's Bay Company.* Toronto: Macmillan, 1976.

Gooderham, George H. "Peter Erasmus." *The Alberta Historical Review,* Vol. 36, 1988.

Gordon, Andrew. *The Rules of the Game: Jutland and British Naval Command.* Annapolis, Maryland: Naval Institute Press, 1996.

Gryba, E.M. & D.A. Barnett. *Sibbald Flat: A Record of 11,000 Years of Human Utilization of the Southern Alberta Foothills.* Edmonton: Alberta Culture, 1981.

Halsey, Francis Whiting. *The Literary Digest History of the World War.* 10 Vol., New York and London: Funk & Wagnalls Company, 1919.

Kauffman, A.J. & W.L. Putnam. *The Guiding Spirit.* Revelstoke, B.C.: Footprint Publishing, 1986.

Kennedy, M.S. (ed) & J.L. Long *The Assiniboines: From the Accounts of the Old Ones.* University of Oklahoma Press, 1961.

Lent, D. Geneva. *West of the Mountains: James Sinclair and the Hudson's Bay Co.* Seattle: University of Washington Press, 1963.

MacEwan, Grant. *Fifty Mighty Men.* Saskatoon: Western Producer Prairie Books, 1982.

MacEwan, Grant. *Colonel James Walker: Man of the Western Frontier.* Saskatoon: Western Producer Prairie Books, 1989.

McGillivray, George B. *Our Heritage: A Brief History of Early Fort William and the Great North West Company.* Thunder Bay: The Times-Journal Commercial Printers, 1970.

McLeod, J.E.A. "Peigan Post and the Blackfoot Trade." *Canadian Historical Review, vol. 24.* Toronto: University of Toronto Press, 1943.

Morton, Arthur S. *Sir George Simpson.* Toronto: J.M. Dent and Sons, 1944.

Oltman, Ruth. *My Valley: the Kananaskis.* Calgary: Rocky Mountain Books, 1997.

Palliser, John. *The Papers of the Palliser Expedition,* 1857-1860. Edited, with an introduction and notes, by Irene M. Spry. Toronto: The Champlain Society, 1968.

Patterson, H.S. "On the Trail of Palliser." *The Beaver Magazine,* March 1937.

Patterson, R.M. *The Buffalo Head.* Toronto: Macmillan, 1961.

Patton, Brian, ed. *Tales from the Canadian Rockies.* Toronto: McClelland & Stewart, 1984.

Pocaterra, George, N. "Among the Nomadic Stoneys." *Alberta Historical Review, vol. II, no.3.* Calgary: Historical Society of Alberta, 1963.

Putnam, W, G.W. Boles, and R.W. Laurilla. *Place Names of the Canadian Alps.* Revelstoke, B.C.: Footprint Publishing, 1990.

Ronaghan, Allen. "The Problem of Maskipiton." *The Alberta Historical Review,* vol. 24., 1976.

Sealey, D. Bruce. *Jerry Potts.* Toronto: Fitzhenry & Whiteside, 1980.

Simpson, George. *Narrative of a journey round the world, during the years 1841 and 1842.* London: H. Colburn, repr. 1983, c1847.

Smith, Cyndi. *Off the Beaten Track.* Jasper, Alberta: Coyote Books, 1989.

Snow, Chief John. *These Mountains are our Sacred Places.* Toronto: Samuel Stevens, 1977.

Spry, Irene M. "Routes Through the Rocky Mountains." *The Beaver Magazine,* Autumn 1963.

Spry, Irene M. *The Palliser Expedition,* 1857-1860. Toronto: Macmillan, 1963; Calgary: Fifth House Ltd., 1995.

Stoney Elders, *The Stonies of Alberta.* Calgary: The Alberta Foundation, 1983.

The Times. *History of the War. 22 Vol.,* London: Printing House Square, 1914-1921.

Thomson, Don W. *Men and Meridians.* Ottawa: Queen's Printer, 1966-69.

Town, Florida. *The North West Company: Frontier Merchants.* Toronto: Umbrella Press, 1999.

Tyrrell., J.B., ed. *David Thompson's Narrative of his Explorations in Western America 1784-1812.* Toronto: The Champlain Society, 1916.

Warre, H.J. *Overland to Oregon in 1845: Impressions of a journey across North America.* Ottawa: Public Archives of Canada, 1976.

Wheeler, A.O. and R.W. Cautley. *Report of the commission appointed to delimit the boundary between the provinces of Alberta and British Columbia.* Ottawa: Office of the Surveyor General, 1917-1955.

Woodman, David C. *Unraveling the Franklin Mystery: Inuit Testimony.* Montreal: McGill-Queen's University Press, 1991.

Whyte, Jon. *Indians of the Rockies.* Banff, Alberta: Altitude Publishing, 1985.

Young, Filson. *With the Battle Cruisers.* London, New York, Toronto and Melbourne: Cassell and Company, Ltd., 1921.

Index

Photograpic Credits

The author would like to acknowledge the following for permission to reproduce their photographs. In many cases high-resolution copies have been scanned from publications from which it is impossible to obtain originals due to elapsed time. Every effort has been made to ensure that these historical photos are in the public domain and have been credited to the publication from which they were scanned.

All other images that are not mentioned were taken by the author himself.

The Times of London History of the War, 20 volumes
56 (bottom), 62 (bottom), 64 (bottom), 80 (bottom), 81(bottom), 82 (bottom),, 83 (bottom), 86, 89, 90 (top), 92 (bottom), 93 (bottom), 95 (top and bottom), 107 (bottom), 114 (bottom), 115 (bottom), 116 (bottom), 117, 120 (bottom), 123, 124 (bottom), 125, 142 (bottom),143 (top),143 (bottom), 144, 145 (bottom), 154 (bottom)

The Literary Digest History of the World War, 10 Volumes
91 (bottom), 92 (middle)

Whyte Museum of the Canadian Rockies
Front cover inset, 16 (NA66-299), 74 (M676 Box 7 album 4)

Glenbow Museum
24 (bottom) (NA-2554-2), 25 (bottom) (NA1075-43), 28 (NA5093-739), 39 (bottom) (NA589-3), 49 (NA2554-1), 53 (NA3148-1), 55 (bottom)

(NA659-44), 60 (bottom) (NA 1847-4), 71 (NA2451-7 L-R),72 (middle) (NA609-1), 77 (top) (NA695-38), 77 (bottom) (NA695-39), 100 (top) (NA695-1), 100 (bottom) (NA695-71), 135 (NA1391-1), 151 (NA265-7), 152 (NA659-50)

National Archives of Canada
Front cover inset, 15 (PA-025521), 21 (C-040850), 34 (PA-026684), 36 (C-002774), 41 (PA-100198), 43 (C-044702), 44 (bottom) (C-000531), 61 (C-017492C), 76 (PA-175933), 103 (C-018619), 106 (PA-002723), 134 (C-031272)

British Columbia Archives
128 (H-05812)

Saskatchewan Archives Board
30

Smithsonian Institution
131

Roger Schmidt
81 (top) (4292), 83 (top) (6-147), 84 (bottom) (6-146), 94 (top) (6-134), 126 ((5-16), 130 (5-21), 150 (3-548)

Esther and Dennis Schmidt
52, 97 (top and bottom)

Douglas Leighton
Front cover photo

Canadian Alpine Journal
39, 79, 93 (M200 AC 383#23), 115 (M200AC383#16)

The Author

Ernie Lakusta's interests have always been science and the mountains. Majoring in the biological sciences, Ernie graduated with a B. Ed. degree in 1966 and a M. Sc. degree in 1970. His research was based in Kananaskis Country and it was during this period that he became an avid hiker, amateur photographer and self-taught naturalist.

To this day, the mountains are his passion and he avails himself of every opportunity to travel off the beaten track with his Krummholz Krew hiking buddies. In *Canmore & Kananaskis History Explorer*, he shares the myths, legends and the fascinating history of the region. Ernie lives in Calgary.